SMP interact

Book C1

CAMBRIDGE
UNIVERSITY PRESS

PUBLISHED BY THE PRESS SYNDICATE OF THE UNIVERSITY OF CAMBRIDGE
The Pitt Building, Trumpington Street, Cambridge, United Kingdom

CAMBRIDGE UNIVERSITY PRESS
The Edinburgh Building, Cambridge CB2 2RU, UK
40 West 20th Street, New York, NY 10011–4211, USA
10 Stamford Road, Oakleigh, Melbourne 3166, Australia
Ruiz de Alarcón 13, 28014 Madrid, Spain
Dock House, The Waterfront, Cape Town 8001, South Africa

http://www.cambridge.org

Printed in the United Kingdom at the University Press, Cambridge

Typeface Minion   *System* QuarkXPress®

A catalogue record for this book is available from the British Library

ISBN 0 521 79860 4 paperback

Typesetting and technical illustrations by The School Mathematics Project
Other illustrations by Robert Calow and Steve Lach at Eikon Illustration
Cover image © Tony Stone Images/Darryl Torckler
Cover design by Angela Ashton

The publishers would like to thank the following for supplying photographs:
page 139   Paul Scruton
page 167   David Cassell
All other photographs by Graham Portlock

We have been unable to trace the copyright holder of the photograph on page 175 (from Robin Fabish, *New Zealand Maori: Culture and Craft* [Auckland: Hodder Moa Beckett, 1995], p. 40), and would be grateful for any information that would enable us to do so.

The authors and publishers would like to thank the staff and pupils of Impington Village College, Cambridge, for their help with the production of this book.

Contents

1 Action and result puzzles   **4**

2 Chocolate   **4**

3 Chance   **5**

4 Symmetry   **17**

5 Multiples and factors   **26**

6 Number grids   **33**

7 Constructions   **43**

8 Comparisons   **50**

9 Fractions   **62**

10 Area   **66**

   Review 1   **75**

11 Inputs and outputs   **77**

12 Decimals   **87**

13 Investigations   **96**

14 Parallel lines   **103**

15 Percentage   **114**

16 Think of a number   **126**

17 Quadrilaterals   **131**

18 Negative numbers   **141**

19 Fair to all?   **145**

   Review 2   **154**

20 Know your calculator   **157**

21 Three dimensions   **164**

22 Finding formulas   **175**

23 Ratio   **182**

24 Using a spreadsheet   **194**

25 Functions and graphs   **199**

   Review 3   **206**

Action and result puzzles

These puzzles involve adding, subtracting, multiplying and dividing.
Doing them will help you

- ◆ carry out these sorts of calculations in your head
- ◆ understand more about what happens when you do these calculations
- ◆ explain your methods to other people and listen to their explanations

• How do you match the cards?

There are several different puzzles.
Try to solve some of them.

Try making up your own puzzles.

 # Chocolate

This will help you

- ◆ solve problems
- ◆ explain your reasoning to other people

③ Chance

This is about games and other situations where the outcome is uncertain because it is a matter of chance.
The work will help you

- ◆ use probability as a measure of likelihood
- ◆ calculate probabilities

A Chance or skill?

Some games are games of skill. Some are games of chance.
Many games involve both chance and skill.

There are three games on sheets 111, 112 and 113.

Before you play a game, see if you can tell from the rules
if it is a game of chance, a game of skill, or a game which
involves both chance and skill.

Then play the game and see if you were right.

Jumping the line

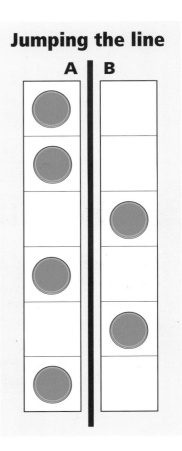

Fours

Line of three

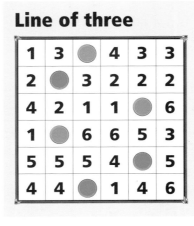

B Fair or unfair?

Three way race

For three players (A, B and C)

Each puts a counter at the start of the track.
Two dice are rolled.

If both numbers are even, A moves forward one space.
If both numbers are odd, B moves forward one space.
If one number is even and one odd, C moves forward
one space.

The first to get to the end of the track is the winner.

- Play the game several times.
  Keep a record of who wins (A, B or C).

Winner	Tally	Number of wins
A		
B		
C		

- Is it a fair game?
  Do all three players have an equal chance
  of winning?

- If you could choose to be A, B or C, which
  would you prefer?
  Or doesn't it matter?

- If you think the game is not fair, can you change it to make it fair?

- Can you explain why it is not fair?

Finish

Start

A   B   C

Rat races

For the whole class

You need sheets 114 and 115.

- Are the races fair?
  Does every rat have an equal
  chance of winning?

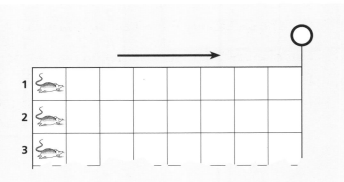

C Probability

Probability is a way of saying how likely something is.

Something which never happens has probability 0.
Something which is certain to happen has probability 1.

Things which have a chance of happening have probabilities between 0 and 1.

Probability scale

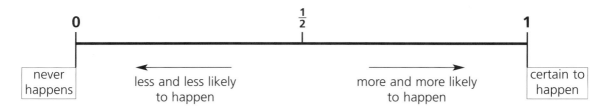

Where would you mark these on the scale?
- The probability that a coin lands heads
- The probability that Rat 1 wins the second rat race
- The probability that the sun will rise tomorrow morning
- The probability that a particular ticket wins the National Lottery

C1 Draw a probability scale like this.

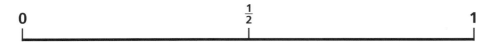

Mark these roughly on your scale with arrows.
(a) The probability that when you roll a dice you get an even number
(b) The probability that when you roll a dice you get a 6

C2 Out of every 1000 babies born, 515 are boys and 485 are girls.
(a) Is a new-born baby more likely to be a boy or a girl?
(b) On the scale you drew, mark roughly the probability that
a new-born baby will be a boy.

D Equally likely outcomes

Sometimes a spinner is used instead of a dice.

This spinner has five equal sections.
You spin the arrow. When it stops it points to a colour.

The five possible colours are called the **outcomes** of a spin.
If the spinner is fair, the five outcomes are **equally likely**.

Suppose you have chosen red.
Red is one of **five** equally likely outcomes.
We say the probability that red will win is $\frac{1}{5}$.

We can also write it as a decimal (0.2) or a percentage (20%).

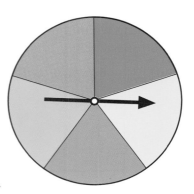

D1 What is the probability that red will win on each of these spinners?

(a) 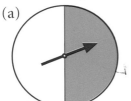 (b) 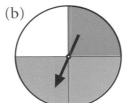 (c) 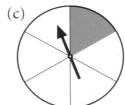 (d)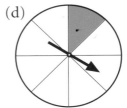

D2 What is the probability that yellow will win on each of these spinners?

(a) 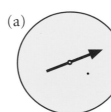 (b)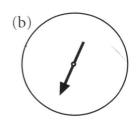

D3 On this spinner, the five sections are equally likely.
Two of the sections are green.
What is the probability that green will win?

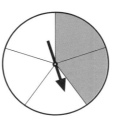

D4 What is the probability that blue will win on each of these spinners?

(a) 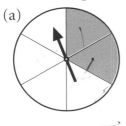 (b) 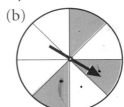 (c) 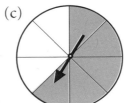 (d)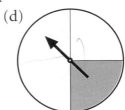

D5 With this spinner, what is the probability that
  (a) yellow wins
  (b) blue wins
  (c) white wins

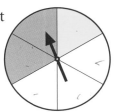

D6 On this spinner, four of the sections are not red.
The probability that red will **not** win is $\frac{4}{5}$.

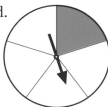

What is the probability that red will **not** win on each of these spinners?

(a) 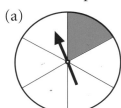 (b) 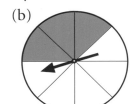 (c) 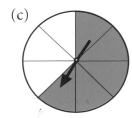 (d)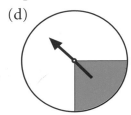

D7 On another spinner, the probability that red will win is $\frac{2}{5}$.
What is the probability that red will not win?

D8 What is the probability that red will not win when the
probability that red wins is
  (a) $\frac{1}{3}$ (b) $\frac{7}{8}$ (c) $\frac{5}{9}$ (d) $\frac{3}{10}$ (e) $\frac{1}{2}$

Odds

The probability of getting red on this spinner is $\frac{1}{4}$.

The probability of getting white is $\frac{3}{4}$.

White is 3 times as likely as red.
Sometimes people say that the 'odds' are 3 to 1 against red.

Odds are used in horse racing and in betting generally.

If you want to tell someone the probability of something,
it is **not** correct to give the odds.
A probability is always a fraction, decimal or percentage.

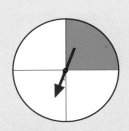

Probability of red = $\frac{1}{4}$
Probability of white = $\frac{3}{4}$

E Equivalent fractions

The probability of getting red on this spinner is $\frac{1}{2}$.

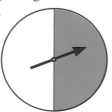

The probability of getting red on this spinner is $\frac{3}{6}$.

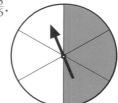

The probabilities of red are equal.

The fractions $\frac{1}{2}$ and $\frac{3}{6}$ are equal, or **equivalent**, fractions.

Here are some other examples of equivalent fractions.

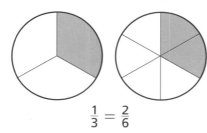

$$\frac{1}{3} = \frac{2}{6}$$

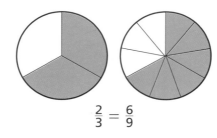

$$\frac{2}{3} = \frac{6}{9}$$

E1 Use these diagrams to help you write down a fraction equivalent to $\frac{1}{4}$.

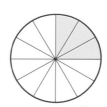

E2 Write down a fraction equivalent to $\frac{1}{5}$.
These diagrams may help.

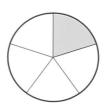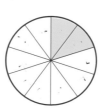

E3 Write down three fractions each equivalent to $\frac{3}{4}$.
These diagrams may help.

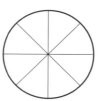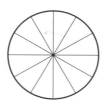

You can make a fraction equivalent to $\frac{2}{3}$ by multiplying the 2 and the 3 by the same number.

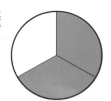

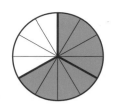

You can reverse the process.
For example, starting with $\frac{8}{12}$ you can divide the 8 and the 12 by 4, to get $\frac{2}{3}$.

*This is called **simplifying** a fraction.*

E4 Simplify each of these fractions.
Make the result as simple as possible (so that you can't go any further).
(a) $\frac{3}{6}$ (b) $\frac{6}{8}$ (c) $\frac{5}{20}$ (d) $\frac{12}{16}$ (e) $\frac{9}{12}$

E5 Simplify each of these fractions as far as possible.
(a) $\frac{10}{40}$ (b) $\frac{9}{24}$ (c) $\frac{8}{12}$ (d) $\frac{9}{21}$ (e) $\frac{4}{20}$

E6 Simplify each of these fractions as far as possible.
One of them cannot be simplified – which one?
(a) $\frac{20}{30}$ (b) $\frac{15}{24}$ (c) $\frac{12}{30}$ (d) $\frac{9}{25}$ (e) $\frac{14}{35}$

*The 'top number' of a fraction is called the **numerator**.*

To simplify a fraction, divide the numerator and denominator by the same number.

*The 'bottom number' is called the **denominator**.*

E7 Some of these fractions can be simplified and some cannot.
Pick out the ones which can be simplified, and simplify them as far as possible.
(a) $\frac{12}{36}$ (b) $\frac{16}{27}$ (c) $\frac{18}{27}$ (d) $\frac{12}{25}$ (e) $\frac{24}{60}$

(f) $\frac{28}{42}$ (g) $\frac{15}{35}$ (h) $\frac{15}{32}$ (i) $\frac{30}{48}$ (j) $\frac{12}{45}$

E8 Simplify as far as possible the fraction $\frac{48}{72}$.

F Choosing at random

There are 100 raffle tickets in a box, numbered from 1 to 100.
A person shuts their eyes, stirs up the tickets and takes one out
without looking.

This is called choosing a ticket **at random**.
Every ticket is equally likely to be chosen.

Rae has bought the tickets with these numbers: 31, 32, 33, 34, 35.

There is only one prize.
The probability that one of Rae's tickets will be chosen is $\frac{5}{100}$, which is equivalent to $\frac{1}{20}$.

F1 There are 50 raffle tickets in a box, numbered from 1 to 50.
One ticket will be drawn at random.
Jodie has ticket number 42.

What is the probability that her number will be drawn?

F2 A box contains 200 raffle tickets numbered from 1 to 200.
One ticket is to be drawn at random.
Justin has the tickets with these numbers: 121, 122, 123, 124.

What is the probability that one of his numbers will be drawn?

F3 A box has 250 raffle tickets in it, and one ticket will be drawn at random.
Pam has bought 10 tickets.

What is the probability that one of her numbers will be drawn?
Write it in the simplest possible way.

F4 Imagine these eight cards are
turned over and shuffled.

You pick a card at random.
What is the probability that you will pick

(a) the number 4   (b) the number 5   (c) an even number

(d) an odd number   (e) a factor of 12   (f) the number 2

(g) a number which is less than 7

F5 In a fairground game there are 100 sticky labels on a board.

Under one of them is a prize token.

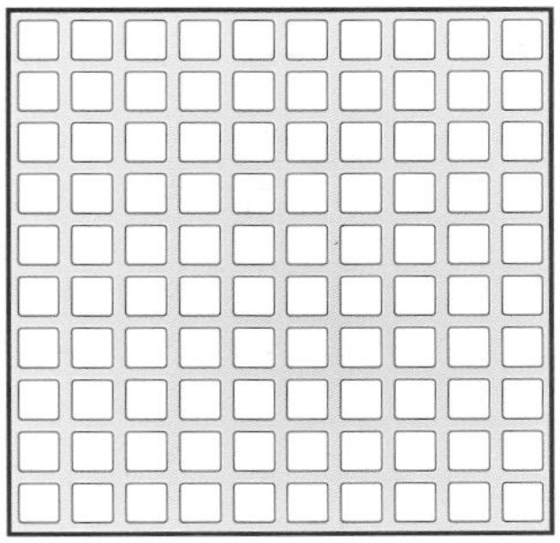

(a) Derek is the first person to have a go.
He chooses a label and peels it off.

What is the probability that
he will win the prize?

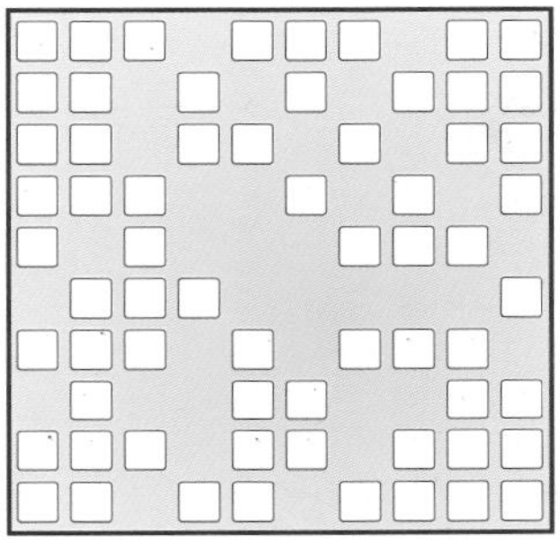

(b) Later the board looks like this.
Derek comes back and
chooses another label.

What is the probability that
he will win this time?

(c) Suppose Derek is unsuccessful.
He has another go.

What is the probability that he will win this time?

F6 Sarah likes red sweets but not green ones.
She can pick a sweet at random from either bag A or bag B.

Which bag should she pick from?

Why?

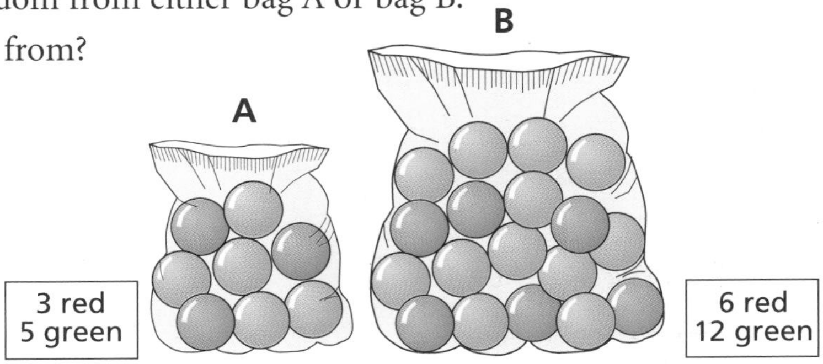

B

A

3 red
5 green

6 red
12 green

F7 Dilesh likes green sweets but not red ones.
He can pick a sweet from either bag C or bag D.

Which bag should he pick from?

Why?

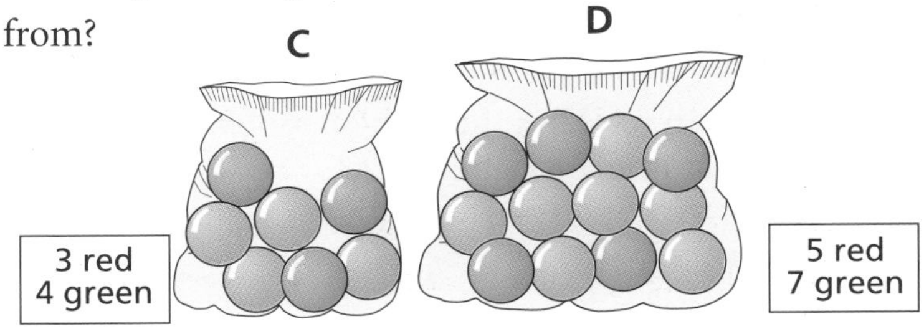

C

D

3 red
4 green

5 red
7 green

G Revisiting games of chance

G1 This is the track for the 'Three way race'.

Two dice are thrown.
If both numbers are even, A moves one space.
If both are odd, B moves one space.
If one is even and one odd, C moves one space.

(a) Make a list of all the different pairs of numbers
   you can get when you throw two dice.
   (You should get 36 pairs altogether.)

(b) How many pairs consist of two even numbers,
   how many of two odd numbers, and how many
   of one even and one odd number?

(c) What does this explain about the game?

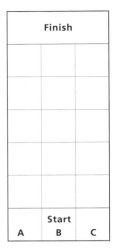

G2 In the 'Second rat race', the rats are numbered from
   1 to 12.
   Two dice are thrown.
   The total tells you which rat moves.

(a) Look again at the list you made for question G1(a).
   How many of the pairs add up to 12?
   How many add up to 11, 10, … etc?

(b) What does this explain about the rat race?

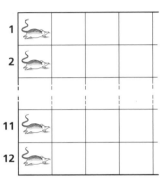

When two dice are thrown, there are 36 possible outcomes.
Each of these outcomes is equally likely.
The probability of each outcome is $\frac{1}{36}$.

From this we can work out the probability of getting, for example,
a total of 8 with the two dice.
These are the outcomes which each give a total of 8:

   2, 6   3, 5   4, 4   5, 3   6, 2

There are 5 of them. So the probability of getting a total of 8 is $\frac{5}{36}$.

G3 (a) What is the probability of getting a total of 10 with two dice?

(b) Which total has the highest probability?
   What is its probability?

G4 (a) In how many of the outcomes of two dice are both numbers even?

(b) What is the probability of throwing two even numbers?

(c) What is the probability of throwing two odd numbers?

(d) What is the probability of throwing one even and one odd?

G5 Go through the list of the 36 equally likely outcomes when two dice are thrown. Work out the **product** for each outcome. (For example, the outcome 3, 5 gives a product of 15.)

A two-way table is useful for recording the products.

(a) What is the probability of getting a product of 12 when you throw two dice?

(b) Work out the probability of each of the other products you can get.

(c) What is the probability of getting the product 21?

The product of 3 and 5 is 15.

Dice 2

	1	2	3	4	5	6
6						
5			15			
4						
3						
2						
1						

Dice 1

G6 Jack and Jill play a game. They roll two dice.
If the **difference** between the two numbers is 0, 1 or 2, then Jack wins.
If the difference is 3, 4, or 5, then Jill wins.

(a) Is this a fair game? Explain.

(b) Can you modify the game, still using differences, to make it fair?

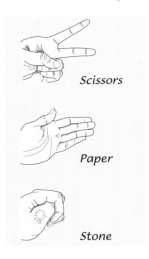

Scissors

Paper

Stone

G7 The game of 'Scissors, paper, stone' is played by two people. They both put one hand behind them and bring it out at the same time. The hand can be showing 'scissors', 'paper' or 'stone'.

Scissors beats paper, paper beats stone and stone beats scissors.
If both players show the same, there is a draw.

(a) Make a list of all the possible outcomes for the pair of players.

(b) Assume that all the outcomes are equally likely. What is the probability of a draw?

G8 Karl has a novel idea for a lottery. Four balls of different colours (red, blue, yellow, green) are put into a bag.
They will be taken out, one at a time, without looking.
People have to guess in which order they will come out.
They have to be exactly right to win.

Jo guesses 'yellow, red, green, blue'.
What is the probability that she will be right?

What progress have you made?

Statement

Evidence

I understand the probability scale.

1. (a) Draw a probability scale.
   What number goes at each end?

   (b) What can you say about something whose probability is 0?

   (c) What can you say about something whose probability is 1?

   (d) Mark with an arrow on your scale the probability that a coin lands tails.

I can work out a probability using equally likely outcomes.

2. What is the probability of getting red on each of these spinners?

   (a) 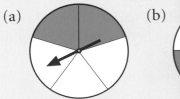   (b)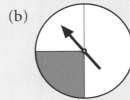

3. A box contains 80 raffle tickets, numbered from 1 to 80.
   Zara has four tickets: 51, 52, 53, 54.
   What is the probability that one of her numbers will be drawn?

I can simplify fractions.

4. Write each of these fractions as simply as possible.

   (a) $\frac{18}{30}$ (b) $\frac{25}{45}$ (c) $\frac{16}{40}$

I can list the equally likely outcomes in a situation involving a pair, and work out probabilities.

5. These two spinners are spun.

   (a) Write down all the equally likely outcomes of the pair of spins.

   (b) What is the probability of getting a total of 5 on the two spinners?

④ Symmetry

This work will help you

◆ recognise rotation symmetry

◆ draw patterns with rotation symmetry

◆ find all the different symmetries in a pattern

A What is symmetrical about these shapes?

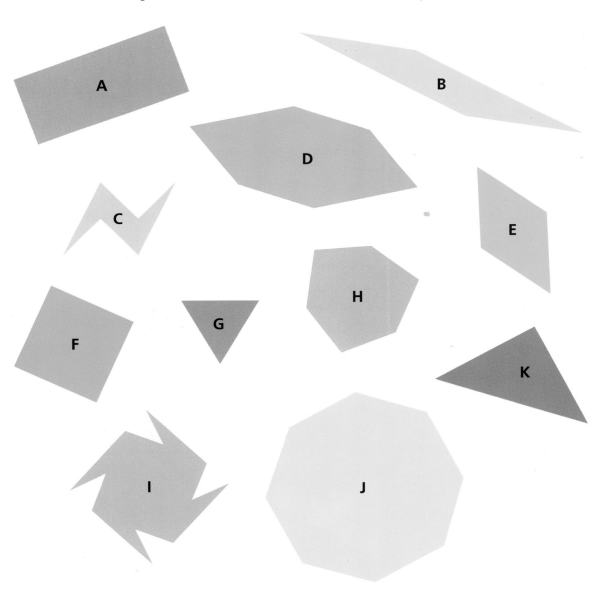

B Rotation symmetry

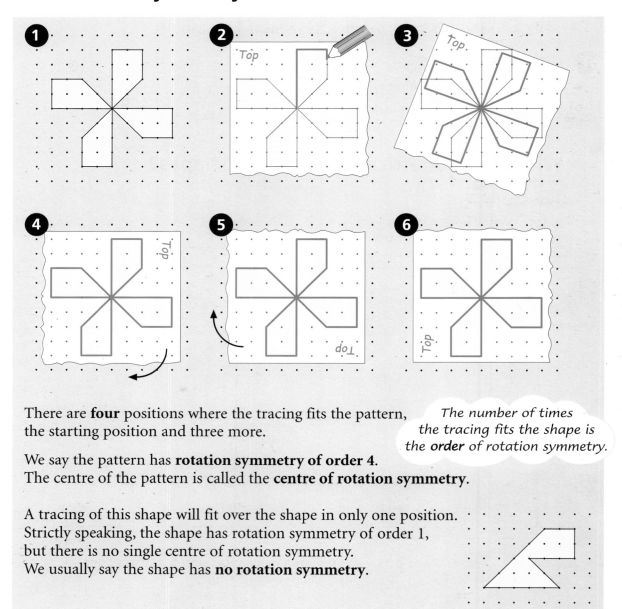

There are **four** positions where the tracing fits the pattern, the starting position and three more.

*The number of times the tracing fits the shape is the **order** of rotation symmetry.*

We say the pattern has **rotation symmetry of order 4**.
The centre of the pattern is called the **centre of rotation symmetry**.

A tracing of this shape will fit over the shape in only one position.
Strictly speaking, the shape has rotation symmetry of order 1,
but there is no single centre of rotation symmetry.
We usually say the shape has **no rotation symmetry**.

B1 You need sheet 117.

Write down the order of rotation symmetry of each design.
Mark the centre of rotation with a dot (unless the order is 1).

C Making designs

C1 Make a design with rotation symmetry of order 4 like this.

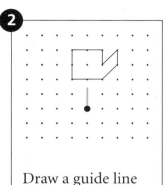 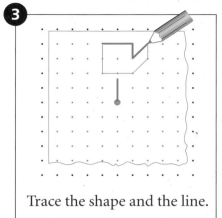

1 Copy this on to square dotty paper.

The large dot will be the centre of rotation symmetry.

2 Draw a guide line from the centre of rotation symmetry.

3 Trace the shape and the line.

4 Rotate the tracing 90°.
Make a copy of the shape.

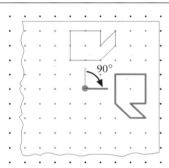

90°

5 Rotate the tracing 90° twice more and copy the shape each time.

C2 On sheet 120, complete each design so it has rotation symmetry of order 4.
Do it without using tracing paper. Then check by tracing.

C3 Copy and complete each pattern so it has rotation symmetry of order 4.

(a) 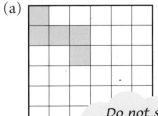 (b) 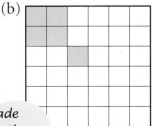 (c)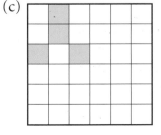

Do not shade more squares than you need to.

19

C4 Make a design with rotation symmetry of order 3 like this.

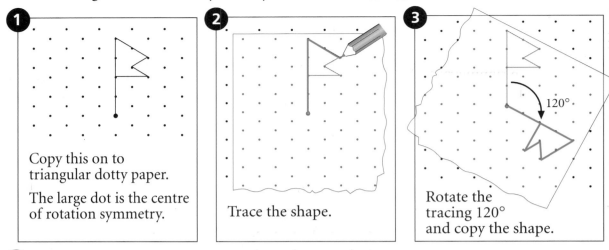

1 Copy this on to triangular dotty paper.

The large dot is the centre of rotation symmetry.

2 Trace the shape.

3 Rotate the tracing 120° and copy the shape.

120°

4 Rotate the tracing 120° once more and copy the shape on to the dotty paper again.

C5 On sheet 121, complete each design so it has rotation symmetry of order 3.
Do it without using tracing paper. Then check by tracing.

C6 Copy and complete each pattern so it has rotation symmetry of order 2.

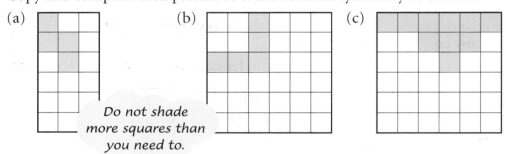

(a)

(b)

(c)

Do not shade more squares than you need to.

C7 Copy and complete each pattern so it has rotation symmetry of order 3.

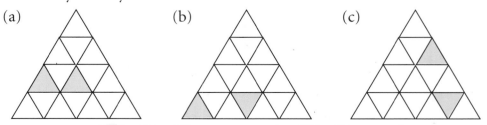

(a)

(b)

(c)

Do not shade more triangles than you need to!

D Rotation and reflection symmetry

From now on, ignore rotation symmetry of order 1.

Some patterns and shapes have rotation symmetry **and** reflection symmetry.

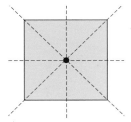

A square has four lines of reflection symmetry and rotation symmetry of order 4.

D1 Copy the shapes below.

For each shape, draw all the lines of symmetry and mark any centre of rotation.

Write the order of rotation symmetry under shapes with rotation symmetry.

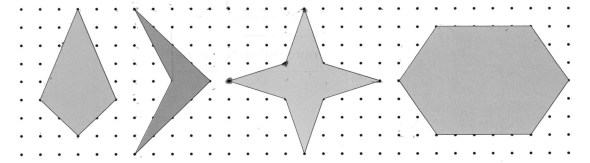

D2 For each design on sheet 122, draw all the lines of symmetry and mark any centre of rotation.

Write the order of rotation symmetry under designs with rotation symmetry.

D3 Four squares are shaded on this 4 by 4 grid.

(a) What is its order of rotation symmetry?

(b) Does it have reflection symmetry?

D4 Find eight different ways of shading four squares on a 4 by 4 grid to make a pattern with rotation symmetry.

What is the order of rotation symmetry of each pattern? Show any lines of symmetry on your patterns.

D5 On a 3 by 3 grid, shade four squares to make a pattern with

(a) rotation symmetry and reflection symmetry

(b) rotation symmetry but no reflection symmetry

(c) reflection symmetry but no rotation symmetry

(d) no rotation symmetry or reflection symmetry

E Pentominoes

A pentomino is a shape made from five squares touching edge to edge.

This pentomino has no rotation symmetry and one line of symmetry.

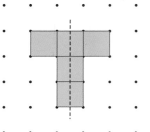

E1 Find a different pentomino with no rotation symmetry and one line of symmetry.

E2 Draw a pentomino with

(a) no rotation symmetry and no lines of symmetry

(b) four lines of symmetry and rotation symmetry of order 4

(c) rotation symmetry of order 2 and no lines of symmetry

(d) two lines of symmetry and rotation symmetry of order 2

E3 This shape is made from two pentominoes.

They do not overlap.

It has rotation symmetry of order 2 but no lines of symmetry.

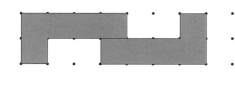

(a) With the same two pentominoes and with no overlapping,

(i) make a different shape with rotation symmetry of order 2 but no lines of symmetry

(ii) make a shape with a line of symmetry but no rotation symmetry (you can flip over a pentomino)

(iii) make a shape with two lines of symmetry and rotation symmetry of order 2

(b) With four of these pentominoes and with no overlapping, make a design with rotation symmetry of order 4.

Does your design have any lines of symmetry?

E4 Choose one of the pentominoes you drew in E1 or E2.

With two or more copies of your pentomino, try to make a design with

(a) reflection symmetry but no rotation symmetry

(b) rotation symmetry but no reflection symmetry

(c) reflection symmetry and rotation symmetry

F Infinite patterns

This is part of an **infinite** pattern. It extends in all directions.

Some of its lines of symmetry and centres of rotation symmetry are marked.

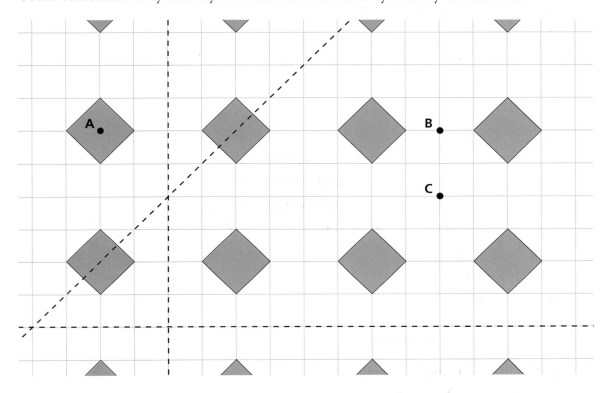

There is a copy of the pattern above on sheet 123.

- Make, or imagine, a tracing of the pattern.
  You have to think of the tracing as infinite.

  The tracing is rotated about centre A.
  In how many positions will it fit the pattern?
  So what is the order of rotation symmetry about A?

- What is the order of rotation symmetry about B? about C?

- Find as many other lines and centres of symmetry as you can.

The sheets you use for questions F1 and F2 will be needed later.

F1 You need sheet 123.
   On the second pattern mark as many lines and centres of symmetry as you can.
   Label each centre with its order of rotation symmetry

F2 Do the same for the patterns on sheet 124.

G Translation

Make, or imagine, a tracing of the infinite pattern below.

If the tracing slides 4 units to the left, as shown by arrow **a**, it will
fit the pattern again. (Remember the pattern and tracing are infinite.)

A sliding movement without any rotation is called a **translation**.

Arrows **b** and **c** show other translations that make the tracing fit the pattern.

Translation **c** can be described as '4 units left, 4 units up'.

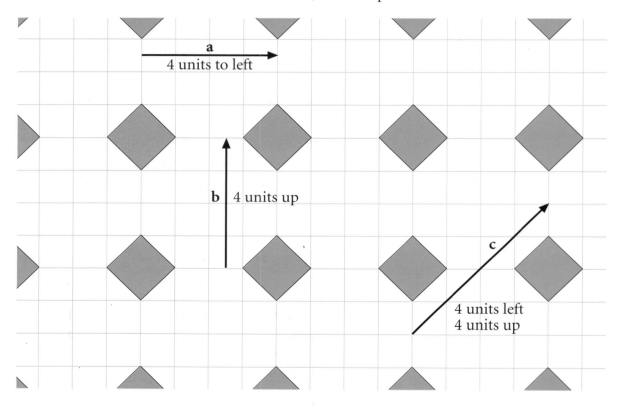

G1 Karl says that the translation which moves
   triangle A to triangle B is '3 right, 1 up'?
   Is he correct? If not, what should it be?

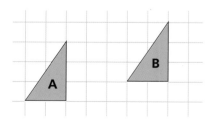

G2 On each pattern on sheet 123, draw arrows to show three different translations
   that make a tracing fit the pattern.

G3 Do the same for the patterns on sheet 124.

What progress have you made?

Statement

I can find centres and orders of rotation symmetry and lines of symmetry.

Evidence

1 (a) Sketch these patterns, mark the centres of rotation and, next to each sketch, write its order of rotation symmetry.

(b) Show all lines of symmetry on your diagrams.

I can design patterns with rotation symmetry.

2 (a) Copy and complete pattern A so it has rotation symmetry of order 4.

(b) Copy and complete pattern B so it has rotation symmetry of order 3.

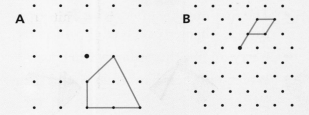

I can draw shapes with given symmetry.

3 On a 4 by 4 grid of squares, shade eight squares to make a pattern with rotation symmetry of order 4 but no reflection symmetry.

I can describe a translation.

4 This is part of an infinite pattern.

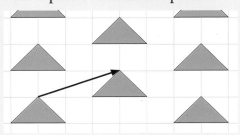

(a) The arrow shows a translation that makes a tracing of the pattern fit the pattern. Describe this translation.

(b) Describe a different translation that makes a tracing fit the pattern.

25

⑤ Multiples and factors

This work will help you
- ◆ understand multiples, factors and prime numbers
- ◆ find the prime factorisation of a number
- ◆ use powers
- ◆ find the highest common factor and lowest common multiple of a pair of numbers

A The sieve of Eratosthenes

You need a hundred square (sheet 134).

- Put a ring round 2. Then cross out all the other multiples of 2.
- The first number after 2 that isn't crossed out is 3. Ring 3. Then cross out all the other multiples of 3. (Some will be crossed out already. Why?)
- The first number after 3 that isn't crossed out is 5. Ring 5. Then cross out all the other multiples of 5.
- Carry on like this as far as you can.
- Which numbers have rings round them?

B Factor pairs

Here are all the factors of 20.
They are paired off, so that each pair multiplies to make 20.

B1 Draw a diagram, similar to the one above, for the factors of
   (a) 12   (b) 18   (c) 24   (d) 30

B2 (a) Draw a diagram for factors of 36. What is special about it?
   (b) Find three more numbers with similar diagrams.
        What is special about these numbers?

B3 Draw a diagram for 17. What is special about it? Why?

B4 You can tell whether a number has 3 as a factor by adding up its digits.
   If the total is divisible by 3, then so is the original number. (Try it!)

   Can you find a way of telling whether a number has each of these as factor?
      10, 5, 4, 6, 9

C Factor trees

For class or group discussion

Start with the number 48.

Think of a pair of factors that make 48, for example, 4 and 12.

Now do the same for 4 and 12.

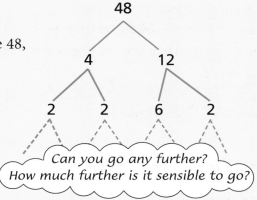

Can you go any further?
How much further is it sensible to go?

The diagram is called a **factor tree**.
(Unlike ordinary trees it grows downwards.)

C1 (a) A factor tree for 40 can be started in different ways. Here is one way. Copy and finish the tree.

(b) Now start the tree in different ways and finish each one. Do all the trees end with the same numbers?

C2 Make factor trees for

    (a) 28   (b) 30   (c) 72   (d) 100

C3 What are the missing numbers in each of these factor trees?

(a) 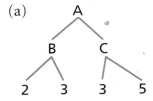   (b)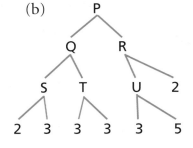

(c) 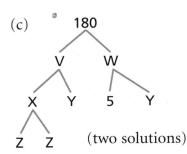   (two solutions)   (d)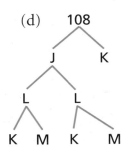

27

D Prime factorisation

When a factor tree is finished, the numbers at the
ends of the branches are all prime numbers.
They multiply together to make the starting number.

$$60 = 2 \times 3 \times 2 \times 5$$

The prime factors are usually written in order of size:

$$60 = 2 \times 2 \times 3 \times 5$$

This called the **prime factorisation** of 60.

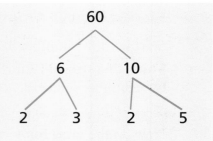

D1 Use the factor trees you have made to help you write down
the prime factorisation of each of these numbers.

(a) 40   (b) 28   (c) 30   (d) 72   (e) 100

Powers

You know that 3^2 means 3×3.

3^2 is also read as '3 to the power 2'.

3^3 ('3 to the power 3') means $3 \times 3 \times 3$.

3^4 means $3 \times 3 \times 3 \times 3$, and so on.

Powers are useful when writing prime factorisations.

For example, the prime factorisation of 200 is $2 \times 2 \times 2 \times 5 \times 5$.

Using powers, this can be written $2^3 \times 5^2$.

D2 Write each of these using powers.

(a) $5 \times 5 \times 5$ (b) $3 \times 3 \times 3 \times 3 \times 3$ (c) $7 \times 7 \times 7$

(d) $2 \times 2 \times 2 \times 3 \times 3$ (e) $3 \times 3 \times 5 \times 5 \times 5 \times 7 \times 7$

D3 Find the prime factorisation of each of these numbers
and write it using powers.

(a) 16   (b) 50   (c) 48   (d) 80   (e) 84   (f) 54

D4 Use a calculator to help you find the prime factorisation
of each of these numbers.

(a) 192   (b) 605   (c) 675   (d) 936

E Lowest common multiple

The **lowest common multiple** (**LCM**) of two numbers is the lowest number which is a multiple of both numbers.

For example, the multiples of 8 are: 8, 16, 24, 32, 40, ...
The multiples of 12 are: 12, 24, 36, ...

The lowest number which appears in both lists is 24.
So 24 is the LCM of 8 and 12.

E1 (a) Make a list of the first few multiples of 4 and a list of the first few multiples of 6.

(b) What is the LCM of 4 and 6?

E2 Find the LCM of
(b) 8 and 10   (b) 6 and 20   (c) 15 and 20   (d) 10 and 12

E3 Find the LCM of 4, 9 and 12.

Finding the LCM using prime factorisation

Example   Find the LCM of 12 and 30.

First find the prime factorisation of each number.
$12 = 2 \times 2 \times 3$
$30 = 2 \times 3 \times 5$
The LCM must contain all the factors of 12: that's $2 \times 2 \times 3$ so far.

It must contain all the factors of 30.
We have 2×3 already, but we need the 5 as well.

So the LCM is $2 \times 2 \times 3 \times 5$, which is **60**.

E4 Use these prime factorisations to find the LCM of 12 and 28.
$12 = 2 \times 2 \times 3$ $28 = 2 \times 2 \times 7$

E5 Write down the prime factorisations of 18 and 45, and use them to find the LCM of 18 and 45.

E6 Use prime factorisation to find the LCM of
(a) 25 and 30   (b) 30 and 48   (c) 16 and 24   (d) 18 and 42   (e) 24 and 28

F Highest common factor

The **highest common factor** (**HCF**) of two numbers is the highest number which is a factor of both numbers.

For example, the factors of 12 are 1, 2, 3, 4, 6, 12.
The factors of 30 are 1, 2, 3, 5, 6, 10, 15, 30.

The highest number which appears in both lists is **6**.
6 is the HCF of 12 and 30.

F1 (a) Make a list of all the factors of 16 and a list of all the factors of 20.

(b) What is the HCF of 16 and 20?

F2 Find the HCF of

(a) 8 and 20   (b) 20 and 30   (c) 30 and 45   (d) 10 and 16

F3 Find the HCF of 8, 12 and 20.

Finding the HCF using prime factorisation

Example Find the HCF of 48 and 60.

First find the prime factorisation of each number.

$48 = 2 \times 2 \times 2 \times 2 \times 3$

$60 = 2 \times 2 \times 3 \times 5$

The HCF is the product of the group of numbers which appear in **both** factorisations. This is the group $2 \times 2 \times 3$.

So the HCF is $2 \times 2 \times 3$, which is **12**.

F4 Use these prime factorisations to find the HCF of 36 and 54.

$36 = 2 \times 2 \times 3 \times 3$ $54 = 2 \times 3 \times 3 \times 3$

F5 Write down the prime factorisations of 32 and 80, and use them to find the HCF of 32 and 80.

F6 Use prime factorisation to find the HCF of

(a) 45 and 60   (b) 32 and 48   (c) 24 and 64   (d) 18 and 42   (e) 25 and 28

F7 Find   (a) the LCM of 16 and 30   (b) the HCF of 45 and 120

(c) the HCF of 18 and 48   (d) the LCM of 18 and 48

F8 Find   (a) the LCM of 36 and 10   (b) the HCF of 36 and 300

           (c) the HCF of 28 and 42   (d) the HCF of 150 and 120

F9 Find   (a) the LCM of 12, 15 and 16   (b) the HCF of 60, 84 and 36

G Testing for prime numbers

Suppose you think that 1927 might be a prime number.

If it is, that means it is not divisible by 2, or 3, or 5, or 7, or any prime number.

Try 2: $1927 \div 2 = 963.5$ **2**   **963.5**
1927 is not divisible by 2.

Try 3: $1927 \div 3 = 642.333...$ **3**   **642.333...**
1927 is not divisible by 3.

Try 5: $1927 \div 5 = 385.4$ **5**   **385.4**
1927 is not divisible by 5.

Try 7: $1927 \div 7 = 275.285...$ **7**   **275.285**
1927 is not divisible by 7.

G1 Continue the process and find out whether 1927 is prime.

G2 Find out if 1931 is a prime number.

Do you have to try every prime number up to 1931?

If not, how far do you need to go? (The diagrams above may be helpful.)

G3 'If n is any whole number, then $n^2 + n + 17$ is a prime number.'

Test the truth of this statement for $n = 1, 2, 3, 4, 5, \ldots$

Can you find a value of n for which $n^2 + n + 17$ is not a prime number?

G4 Multiply the first four prime numbers together and add 1.
Is the result a prime number?

Try multiplying the first five, six, … prime numbers together and adding 1.
Is the result always prime?

H Clue-sharing

This activity is described in the teacher's guide.

I Problems

I1 Four bell-ringers ring their bells in this way:

Peter: every 8 seconds   Jane: every 9 seconds

Imran: every 12 seconds   Kelly: every 15 seconds

If they all start at the same time, how long will it be before all four bells ring simultaneously?

I2 The prime factorisation of 240 is $2^4 \times 3 \times 5$.

How can this be used to find **all** the factors (prime and non-prime) of 240?

How many factors does 240 have altogether?

*I3 (a) Find a number greater than 1, which leaves a remainder of 1 when it is divided by 2, by 3, by 4, by 5 and by 6.

(b) Find a number which leaves a remainder of

1 when divided by 2,   2 when divided by 3,

3 when divided by 4,   4 when divided by 5,

5 when divided by 6.

How many numbers are there like this which are less than 1000?

What progress have you made?

Statement	Evidence
I can make a factor tree.	1 Make a factor tree for (a) 45 (b) 60
I can find the prime factorisation of a number.	2 Find the prime factorisation of (a) 96 (b) 8580
I can use powers.	3 Write the prime factorisation of 96 using powers.
I can find the lowest common multiple and the highest common factor of a pair of numbers.	4 Find the LCM of 8 and 14.
	5 Find the HCF of 30 and 75.

⑥ Number grids

This is about number grids and algebra.
The work will help you

◆ solve problems and investigate patterns on a number grid
◆ simplify expressions
◆ use algebra to investigate rules

A Square grids

An introductory activity is described in the teacher's guide.

This number grid uses the rules '+ 6' across (⟶)
and '+ 2' down (↓).

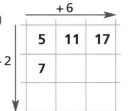

● Copy and complete the grid.

A1 (a) Draw three different sized square grids
that use the rules '+ 6' across and '+ 2' down.
Choose a different number for each top left
corner and complete the grids.

(b) For your grids, find a rule to go diagonally
from one number to another.
Make sure your rule works for all the grids.
Explain how you found your rule.

(c) Use your rule to work out the numbers for the shaded
squares in this grid.

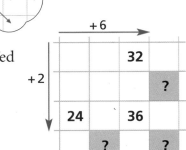

A2 (a) Copy and complete these number grids
to three squares in each direction.

(i)   (ii)   (iii)

(b) For each grid, find a rule to go diagonally (↘) from one number
to another and explain how you found your rule.

33

A3 What are the diagonal rules for these grids? (a)   (b)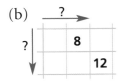

A4 Find some pairs of across and down rules that fit these grids.

What do you notice?

(a)   (b)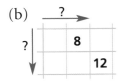

B Grid puzzles

B1 For each puzzle, work out the number in the shaded square.

(a) 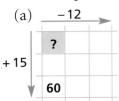 (b) 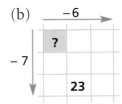 (c)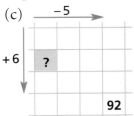

B2 Work out the missing rules in these puzzles.

(a) 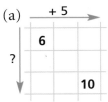 (b) 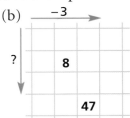 (c)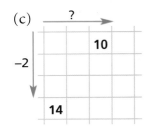

B3 Find the across and down rules for each of these number grid puzzles.

(a) 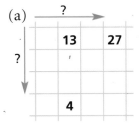 (b) 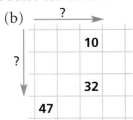 (c)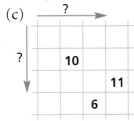

B4 Which of the puzzles in B3 did you find most difficult? Why?

*****B5** Find the missing rules in these puzzles.

(a) 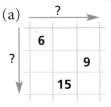 (b) 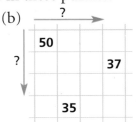 (c) 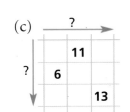 (d)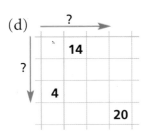

C Algebra on grids

You can use letters for numbers in the top left square.

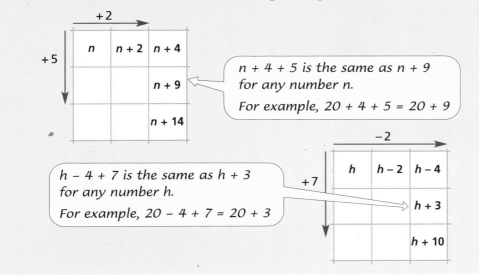

n + 4 + 5 is the same as n + 9 for any number n.

For example, 20 + 4 + 5 = 20 + 9

h – 4 + 7 is the same as h + 3 for any number h.

For example, 20 – 4 + 7 = 20 + 3

C1 Copy and complete these grids to four squares in each direction.

(a)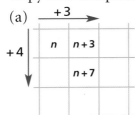

(b)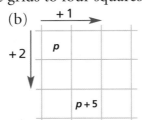

(c)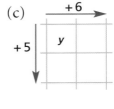

C2 For each grid in C1, work out the number in the bottom right square when the number in the top left square is 100.

C3 Find rules for these grids.

(a)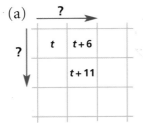

(b)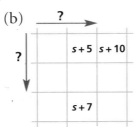

(c)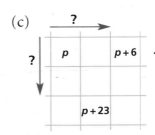

C4 Copy and complete these grids to four squares in each direction.

(a)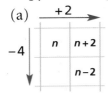

(b)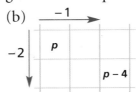

(c)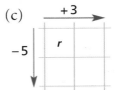

35

C5 For each grid in C4, find the number in the top left square when the number in the bottom right square is 50.

C6 Write each of these in a simpler way.
  (a) $f + 3 + 5 + 3$ (b) $y + 4 + 4 + 4$ (c) $x + 2 + 1 + 2 + 1$
  (d) $z - 5 - 5$ (e) $p + 4 - 3$ (f) $m + 2 - 5$
  (g) $q + 2 + 2 - 1$ (h) $w - 4 - 1 - 9$ (i) $h + 1 - 8 + 5 + 7$

C7 A letter can stand for a number in any position on a grid. Copy and complete this grid to three squares in each direction.

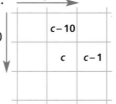

C8 Copy and complete these grids to four squares in each direction.
  (a)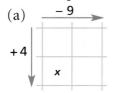

  (b)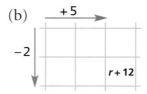

  (c)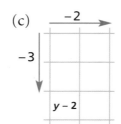

C9 Find the rules for these grids.
  (a)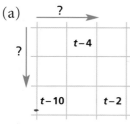

  (b)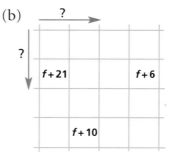

  (c)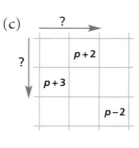

*C10 What are the missing rules for these grids?
  (a)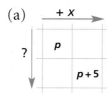

  (b)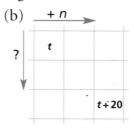

36

D Grid investigations

D1 Suneet uses different numbers in his rules.
He adds the numbers in opposite corners on his grids.
This is one of his grids.

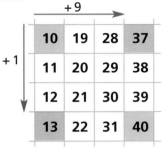

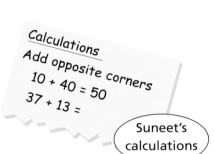

Calculations
Add opposite corners
10 + 40 = 50
37 + 13 =

Suneet's calculations

(a) Copy and complete Suneet's calculations.

(b) Make some more number grids that use the rules
'+ 9' and '+ 1', and add the opposite corners.

(c) What do you notice about the opposite corners totals
on your number grids? Can you explain this?

D2 Choose your own rules and make some number grids.
Investigate adding opposite corners on your grids.

D3 These grids use the rules '+ 2' and '+ 1'.

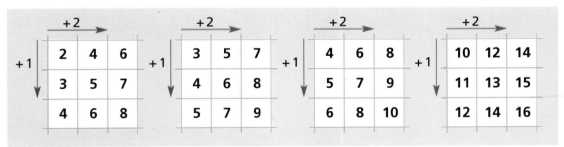

(a) Copy and complete the opposite corners table
for these grids.

(b) Draw some more grids like this and include
the results for your grids in the table.

(c) Find a rule that links the opposite corners total
and the top left number.

(d) What is the opposite corners total when
the number in the top left square is 100?

Opposite corners table	
Top left number	Opposite corners total
2	10
3	12
4	
10	

D4 Investigate opposite corners totals for your own sets of grids.

E Using algebra

Sue uses algebra to investigate her grids.

I use n for the top left number.

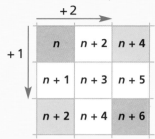

Adding opposite corners

blue corners: n + n + 6
              = 2n + 6

pink corners: n + 2 + n + 4
              = n + n + 2 + 4
              = 2n + 6

> $n + n + 6 = 2n + 6$
> for any value of n.
> So $n + n + 6$ and $2n + 6$
> are called **equivalent expressions**.

The totals are both equivalent to 2n + 6.
So I know that

- the totals will be equal no matter what n is
- to find the total I can use the rule 'multiply n by 2 and add 6'

> $n + 2 + n + 4 = 2n + 6$
> for any value of n.
> So $n + 2 + n + 4$ and $2n + 6$
> are also equivalent
> expressions.

For example, if the top left number is 50,
then the total will be (50 × 2) + 6 = 106.

To check Sue's result, complete this grid
and find the opposite corners total.

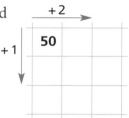

E1

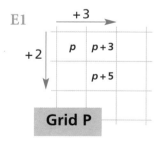

Grid P

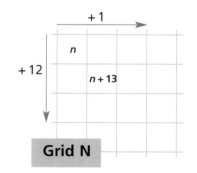

Grid N

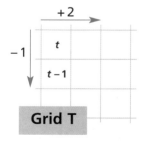

Grid T

Do this for each grid.

(a) Copy and complete it.

(b) Find the total of each pair of opposite corners.

(c) Are the opposite corners totals equal?

(d) Find the opposite corners total if the top left number is 100.

E2 Find four pairs of equivalent expressions.

A $n + 5 + n + 1$

B $2n - 8$

C $n + n + 3 + n + 3$

D $n - 5 + n + 3$

E $3n + 6$

G $n - 6 + n - 2$

I $2n + 6$

F $2n + 4$

H $2n - 2$

E3 Explain the mistake this pupil has made.

When n = 3   2n + 5 = (2 x 3) + 5
                    = 11
              n + 8 = 3 + 8
                    = 11

Not correct, Jake

So 2n + 5 and n + 8 are equivalent expressions.

E4 Write each of these in a simpler way.

(a) $p + p + 6$

(b) $y + 4 + y + 5$

(c) $q + 8 + q + q$

(d) $t + 1 + 3 + t + t$

(e) $x + 2 + x - 1$

(f) $r + r - 3 + r + 9$

(g) $w - 4 + w - 5$

(h) $j + 8 + j - 9$

(i) $h + 1 + h + h - 3$

E5 The diagonals of this number grid are shaded.

Investigate adding the numbers on the diagonals of number grids. Use algebra to explain your conclusions.

+4 →

+3 ↓

25	29	33	37
28	32	36	40
31	35	39	43
34	38	42	46

E6 Find some different pairs of rules that give this grid an opposite corners total of $2t + 30$.

? →

? ↓   t

F Using multiplication

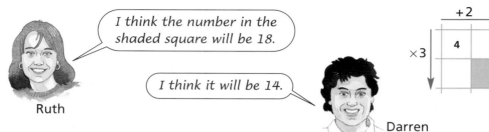

I think the number in the shaded square will be 18.

Ruth

I think it will be 14.

Darren

F1 (a) Who do you think is correct?

(b) Is it possible to make a number grid that uses the rules '+ 2' and '× 3'?
Explain your answer carefully.

F2 Ruth uses the rules '× 5' and '× 3' to make a grid.

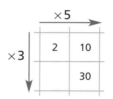

(a) Copy and complete her grid to three squares in each direction.

(b) Explain why it is possible to make a grid that uses the rules '× 5' and '× 3'.

F3 Decide if it is possible to make number grids with each pair of rules.

(a) '− 7' and '× 5'   (b) '× 2' and '× 3'   (c) '+ 8' and '÷ 4'

(d) '÷ 2' and '÷ 4'   (e) '× 6' and '÷ 2'

F4 Copy and complete each grid to three squares in each direction.

(a)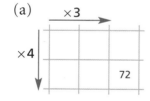

(b)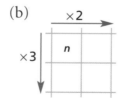

(c)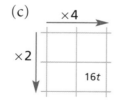

F5 Jack and Tom are investigating this grid.
They decide to multiply opposite corners.

Jack writes:

$$4y \times 25y = 100y$$

Tom writes:

$$4y \times 25y = 100y^2$$

×5	×2		
	y	$2y$	$4y$
	$5y$	$10y$	$20y$
	$25y$	$50y$	$100y$

Which of them is correct?
Give a reason for your answer.

F6 Write each of these in a simpler way.

    (a) $a \times 2$ (b) $2a \times a$ (c) $2a \times 3a$ (d) $3a \times 3a$

    (e) $x \times 5x$ (f) $2x \times 5x$ (g) $5x \times 5x$ (h) $3 \times 4x \times 3x$

F7 Find five pairs of equivalent expressions.

A $12n^2$ B $2 \times 6n$ C $7n$ D $2n \times 6n$ E $6n + 2n$

F $4n + 3n$ G $2n \times 4n$ H $8n$ I $2n^2 + 6n^2$ J $12n$

F8 Write each of these in a simpler way.

    (a) $2p \times 3p$ (b) $2p + 3p$ (c) $2p \times 3$ (d) $3t \times t$

    (e) $3t \times 5t$ (f) $3 \times 5t$ (g) $t \times 5t$ (h) $2x \times 3x \times 4$

    (i) $2x \times 3 \times 4x$ (j) $y \times 4y \times 5$ (k) $5y \times 3 \times y$ (l) $4 \times 2y \times 3y$

F9 Explain why $5p + 2r$ cannot be written in a simpler way.

F10 Write each of these in a simpler way where possible.
If it is not possible, write 'cannot be simplified'.

    (a) $4p \times 3$ (b) $4p + 3p$ (c) $4p \times 3p$ (d) $4p + 3$

    (e) $p + 4 + 3$ (f) $p + 4 + p + 3$.   (g) $p + 4 + p - 3$ (h) $3p - 4$

    (i) $m \times 8m$ (j) $m + 8m$ (k) $9m - 3$ (l) $3m + 2 + 4m$

F11 Simplify these expressions where possible.

    (a) $6x - 1 - 4x - 5$ (b) $20 + 2y - 4 + y$ (c) $2w \times 3w$

    (d) $u - 4 + 3u + 8$ (e) $4u + 3v$ (f) $2 \times 3p \times 3p$

    (g) $24q - 5$ (h) $r - 3 + r - 1$ (i) $2s - 5 + s + 2 + s$

F12 Investigate opposite corners and diagonals
for number grids that use only '$\times$' in their rules.

Use algebra to explain your conclusions.

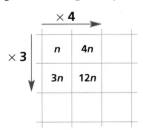

What progress have you made?

Statement	Evidence

I can solve number grid problems.

1 Work out the missing rules in these grids.

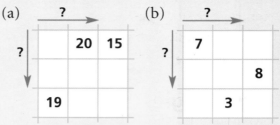

(a)

(b)

I can simplify expressions using addition and subtraction.

2 Write each of these in a simpler way.

(a) $n + 5 + 2$

(b) $p + 10 - 4$

(c) $y - 5 - 2$

(d) $t + 7 - 10$

(e) $h + 4 + h - 1$

(f) $w - 8 + w - 3 + w$

I can use algebra to investigate rules.

3 Jo makes a grid where the across and down rules add and subtract the same number.

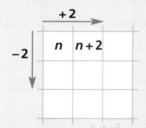

(a) Copy and complete Jo's grid.

(b) Explain why it shows the numbers in one diagonal will always be the same.

(c) What is the opposite corners total for this grid?

(d) What will be the opposite corners total when $n = 6$?

(e) Investigate other grids where the across and down rules add and subtract the same number.

I can simplify expressions involving multiplication.

4 Write each of these in a simpler way.

(a) $t \times t$

(b) $5g \times g$

(c) $3n \times 4n$

(d) $2y \times 5y$

7 Constructions

This is about drawing accurately using ruler and compasses.
The work will help you

◆ construct right angles

◆ bisect a line (divide it in half)

◆ bisect an angle

A Right angles

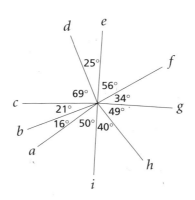

A1 Some of the lines on this diagram are at right angles.

Work out which pairs are at right angles.

A2 Make a sketch of the points of the compass (north, north-east, …).

(a) Jenny is facing west.
She turns through a right angle clockwise.
What direction is she facing now?

(b) Peter is facing south-east.
He turns through a right angle anticlockwise.
What direction is he facing now?

(c) Amal is facing north-west.
She turns through a right angle clockwise.
What direction is she facing now?

A3 This is a sketch of a pattern.
Use a set square to draw it accurately on plain paper.

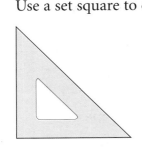

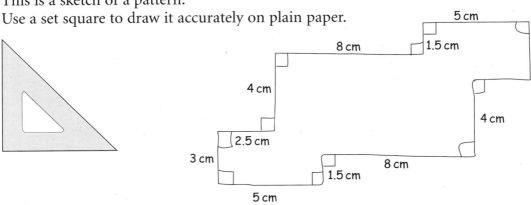

In mathematics, 'line' nearly always means 'straight line'.
A line goes on indefinitely in both directions.

a line

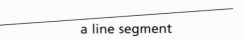

The proper name for a piece of line of a definite
length is **line segment**.
But the word 'segment' can usually be left out
without causing confusion.

a line segment

Lines which are at right angles to each other
are said to be **perpendicular** to each other.

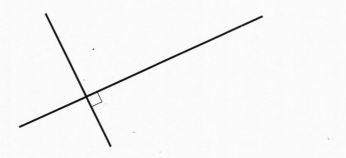

Line segments can be perpendicular
even when they don't meet.

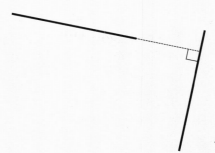

A4 Line segment *a* is perpendicular to *b*.
Check this with a set square.

Some other pairs of line segments are
perpendicular. Find the pairs.
Try to decide without a set square.
Then check with the set square.

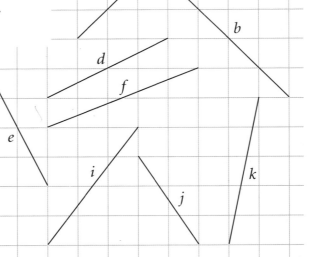

B From a point to a line

In this diagram, *r* is a straight road
and H is the position of a house.

A path is to be made from the house
to the road. It must be as short as possible.

Describe where the path should go.

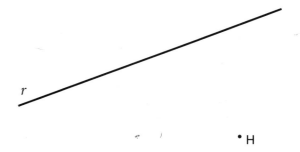

B1 Follow the instructions on sheet 139.

B2 Copy this diagram on to squared paper.

The pentagon ABCDE is a plan of a field.
So the lines AB, BC and so on are hedges.

Mark this journey on your copy:

> Alex starts at A.
> She walks to hedge CD by
> the shortest route.
> From there she walks to hedge AB by
> the shortest route.
> Then she walks to hedge AE by
> the shortest route.

What are the coordinates of
the point she gets to?

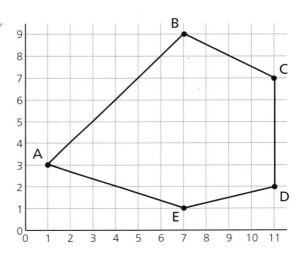

B3 Draw an equilateral triangle whose sides are 10 cm long.

Pick a point P anywhere inside the triangle.

Measure the distance from P to each side
of the triangle.
Add the three distances together.

Now pick a different position for P inside
the triangle, and do the same.
Then do it again for another position of P
inside the triangle.

What do you find?

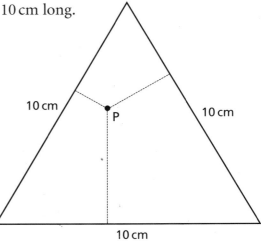

45

C Constructions with ruler and compasses

Drawing a perpendicular from a point to a line

Draw a line.

Mark a point a few centimetres away from it.

With compasses, draw an arc with its centre at the point.

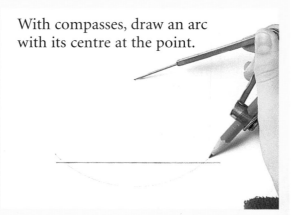

Put the compasses point at one of the points where your arc crosses the line.

Draw an arc below the line.
(You do not have to use the same radius as before.)

Do not alter the radius.

Draw another arc, like this.

The line from your first point to the point where the last pair of arcs cross is perpendicular to your first line.

Can you explain why?

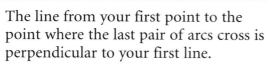

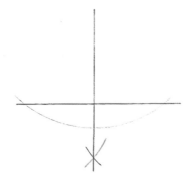

C1 Draw a triangle in the middle of a piece of A4 paper.
Its sides should be between 8 and 16 cm long.
Label the triangle ABC.

Draw the line from A which is perpendicular to BC.
Draw the line from B which is perpendicular to AC.
Draw the line from C which is perpendicular to AB.

What do you notice about the three lines?

Drawing the perpendicular bisector of a line segment

The **perpendicular bisector** of a line segment divides the segment in half
and crosses the line at right angles.

1 Draw a line segment. Draw an arc about this big with its centre at one end of the segment.	**2** Keep your compasses the same radius. Draw an arc with its centre at the other end of the segment.	**3** Draw a line through the points where the two arcs cross. This is the perpendicular bisector of the original segment.

 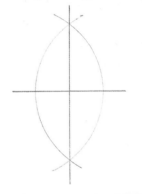

C2 Draw a triangle on A4 paper, as in question C1.
Draw the perpendicular bisector of one of the sides of the triangle.
Now do the same for the other two sides.
What do you notice about the three perpendicular bisectors?

C3 Draw a right-angled triangle ABC, with the right angle at B.
Draw the perpendicular bisectors of AB and of BC.
Where do they meet?

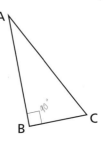

Bisecting an angle

Draw an angle.
Draw an arc with its centre at the vertex of the angle.

Draw two arcs of the same radius from the points where your first arc crosses the arms of the angle.

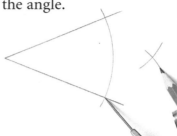

Draw the line which bisects the angle.

Can you explain why it bisects the angle?

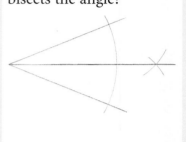

C4 Draw a triangle on A4 paper, as in the previous questions.

Draw the bisector of one of the angles of the triangle.

Now do the same for the other two angles.

What do you notice about the three angle bisectors?

C5 Draw two lines which cross.

Bisect each of the four angles they make.

What do you notice about the angle bisectors? Explain.

Drawing a perpendicular to a line from a point on it

Draw a line and mark a point on it.
Draw arcs with their centres at the marked point.

Draw two arcs of the same radius from the points where your first arcs cross the line.

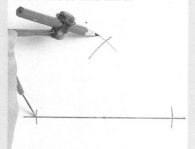

Join the marked point to the point where the last two arcs cross.

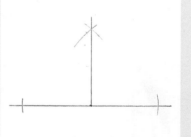

C6 Draw a triangle ABC and extend the sides AB, BC, CA as shown.

At B, construct a line perpendicular to AB.

At C, construct a line perpendicular to BC.

At A, construct a line perpendicular to CA.

Extend each of these lines (if necessary) to make a large triangle.

Measure the angles of this large triangle and the angles of the original triangle.
What do you find?

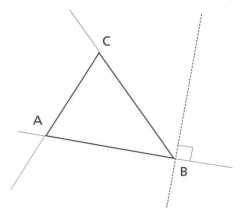

What progress have you made?

Statement	Evidence
I can use ruler and compasses to construct a line perpendicular to a given line, from a point not on it.	1 Draw a line *l* and a point P not on *l*. Construct the line through P perpendicular to *l*.
I can use ruler and compasses to construct a line perpendicular to a given line, from a point on it.	2 Draw a line *l* and mark a point P on *l*. Construct the line through P perpendicular to *l*.
I can use ruler and compasses to draw the perpendicular bisector of a line segment.	3 Draw a line segment AB. Construct the perpendicular bisector of AB.
I can use ruler and compasses to bisect an angle.	4 Draw an angle ABC. Construct the bisector of angle ABC.

8 Comparisons

This work will help you

◆ understand median and range

◆ use them to make comparisons

A Comparing heights

For class or group discussion

- Do you think the girls here are taller or shorter than the boys?
  How do you decide?

- Look at each dot plot below.

  Would you say the girls are taller or shorter than the boys?
  How do you decide?

A

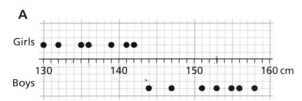

B

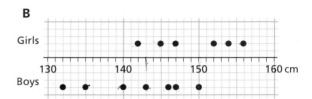

C

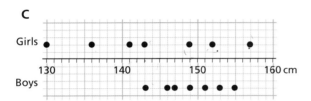

D

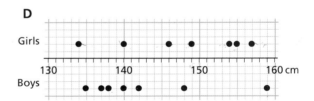

E

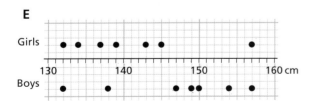

F

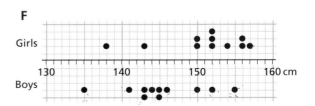

B Median

Here, the top dot plot shows seven girls' heights.
The middle girl's height is marked with an arrow (136 cm).
This is called the **median** height of the group.

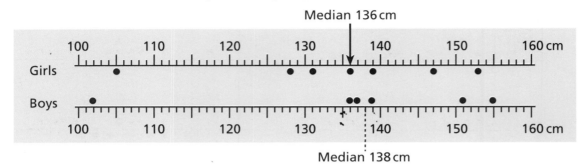

There are six boys' heights so there is no 'middle boy'.
But there is a middle **pair** of boys.

The median height is halfway between the heights of the middle pair.
So the median height is 138 cm.

The median is often used as an 'average' to compare two sets of data.
The median height of the boys is greater than the median height of the girls.

B1 What is the median height of each group shown below?

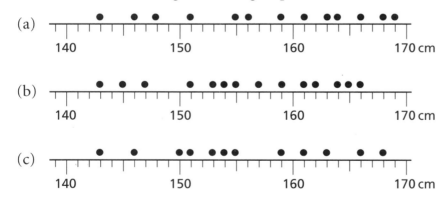

B2 In this group of girls there are two with height 155 cm.

(a) How many girls are there in the group?

(b) Find the dot that represents the middle girl.
Write down the median height.

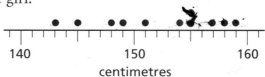

B3 For each of the dot plots on page 51,

   (a) find the median height of the girls

   (b) find the median height of the boys

   (c) use these results to write a statement comparing girls and boys

B4 What is the median height of each of these groups?

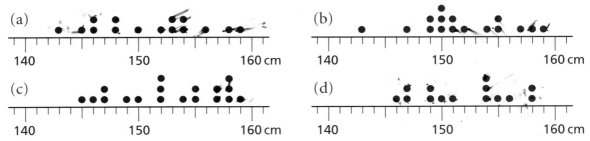

(a)

140   150   160 cm

(b)

140   150   160 cm

(c)

140   150   160 cm

(d)

140   150   160 cm

B5 (a) What is the median weight of
       the group of people shown here?

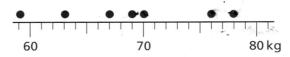

60   70   80 kg

   (b) What would happen to the median weight if the heaviest person
       is replaced by someone even heavier?

   (c) What if the lightest person is replaced by someone even lighter?

   (d) What would happen to the median weight if, after Christmas dinner,
       everyone increased by 1 kg?

B6 Here are the weights, in kg, of the members of a seven-a-side football team.

          63, 54, 70, 65, 58, 52, 60

   (a) Write out these numbers in order of size, smallest first.

   (b) What is the median weight of the team?

> *Always* do this if you are finding a median
> and the numbers are not in order of size.

B7 Find the median of each of these sets of data.

   (a) 156 cm, 148 cm, 161 cm, 139 cm, 152 cm

   (b) 45 kg, 38 kg, 29 kg, 26 kg, 34 kg, 40 kg, 31 kg, 39 kg

B8 Here are the weights, in kg, of a group of baby boys and a group of baby girls.

   Boys   3.2 2.2 1.9 2.8 1.6 2.7 2.2 3.4 1.9 3.0 2.9

   Girls   2.7 3.0 3.1 1.4 2.6 2.6 3.5 2.6 2.8 2.1

   Which group has the greater median weight?

C Range

The two groups shown here have the same median height.
But the girls' heights are more spread out than those of the boys.

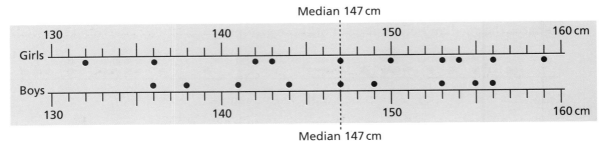

We use the **range** to measure the spread.
The range is the **difference between the largest and smallest**.

The range of the girls' heights is **27 cm** (159 − 132 = 27).

The range of the boys' heights is **20 cm** (156 − 136 = 20).

C1 (a) Work out the range of each group
      of heights shown here.

   (b) Which group has the greatest range?

   (c) Which group has the smallest range?

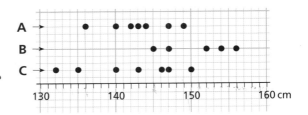

C2 The length of time between phoning for an ambulance and
the ambulance arriving is called the 'response time'.

An ambulance station recorded these response times over a period of one hour.

Time in minutes	10	8	11	6	13	10	4	6	10	7

   (a) What was the longest response time?

   (b) What was the shortest response time?

   (c) Work out the range of the response times.

C3 This table shows information about the
weights of three herds of cows.

	Median	Range
Herd A	525 kg	65 kg
Herd B	545 kg	50 kg
Herd C	510 kg	35 kg

   (a) Which herd is heaviest on the whole?

   (b) In which herd are the weights most spread out?
      How do you know from the table?

   (c) In which herd are the weights least spread out?
      How do you know?

C4 Two friends played a computer game.
They had five goes each. They got a score out of 100 on each go.

Paul

Nicky

(a) Work out the median and range of Paul's scores.

(b) Work out the median and range of Nicky's scores.

Two other friends played the game.
These were the medians and ranges
of their scores.

	Median	Range
Martin	30	28
Carol	84	11

Use the information about **all four people** to copy and complete these sentences.

(c) _____ and _____ both had high scores,
but _____'s scores were the more spread out of the two.

(d) Nicky's scores and _____'s scores were both spread out,
but _____ had the higher scores of the two.

(e) _____ and _____ were both bad players
because they had _____ median scores.

(f) Paul was a consistent player because the range of his scores was _____.

C5 These trees grow on different sides of a hill.

(a) Find the median height and the range of the heights of each group.

(b) Write a couple of sentences comparing the groups.

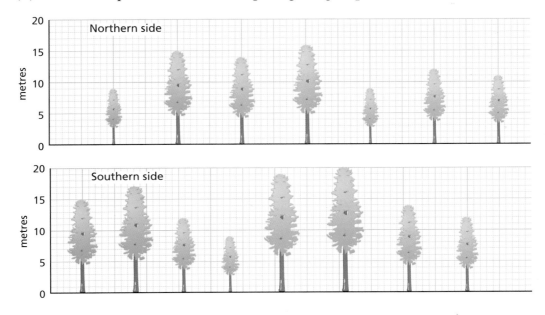

55

C6 Four machines in a factory fill packs with spaghetti.
Each pack should contain 500 g.

The owner operated the machines until each of them had filled nine packs.
She checked the weight of spaghetti in the packs and got these results.

Machine A	500 g	503 g	490 g	495 g	505 g	511 g	485 g	508 g	494 g
Machine B	499 g	496 g	501 g	499 g	497 g	498 g	497 g	499 g	497 g
Machine C	502 g	503 g	502 g	504 g	499 g	502 g	503 g	505 g	502 g
Machine D	499 g	518 g	512 g	521 g	508 g	524 g	514 g	505 g	514 g

(a) Work out the median and range of the weights for each machine.

(b) Which machine was consistent but generally underfilled the packs?

(c) Which was variable and generally overfilled the packs?

(d) Which was consistent and usually overfilled the packs?

(e) How would you describe the remaining machine?

(f) Which machine would the factory owner prefer, if it continued
to work as it did in the test? Give a reason.

D How fast do you react?

For working in pairs

Cut out the reaction timer scale from the sheet 141 and
stick it on to a ruler (or other wooden or plastic strip).

This is how you measure your reaction time.

- Your partner holds the reaction timer at the top.

- You have your thumb and finger ready at the zero mark.

- Your partner drops the reaction timer and you grip it as fast as you can.
  The scale tells you your reaction time in hundredths of a second.

Record the results of ten trials each. Use dot plots if you like.
Compare your results with those of your partner using **median** and **range**.

You could also compare your own reaction times using
your left hand and your right hand.

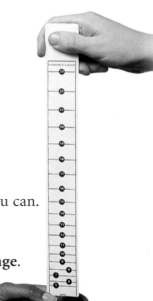

For the whole class

Collect the fastest or the median reaction time of every pupil.

Compare the reaction times of 12-year-olds with those of 13-year-olds.

E Summarising data

The median and range can be used to help summarise a set of data.

The data on the right consists of Claire's reaction times
(in hundredths of a second).

The median reaction time is 17 hundredths of a second.

The shortest time is 8 hundredths of a second.
The longest is 22 hundredths of a second.
The range is 22 − 8, which is 14 hundredths of a second.

Claire's reaction times, in hundredths of a second			
8	12	12	13
16	18	19	19
20	22		

This diagram summarises the data.
It shows the **smallest**, **largest**, **median** and **range**.

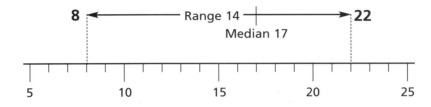

E1 Draw diagrams like the one above to summarise your reaction
times and those of your partner.

Write about any differences you notice.

E2 (a) Here are the reaction times of different people.
Draw a summary diagram for each one.

(i) Janet, 42, a teacher

21, 15, 10, 22, 21, 16, 22, 13, 17, 20, 21

(ii) Linford, 25, a sprinter

13, 10, 14, 10, 9, 7, 13, 11, 11, 10, 7, 6, 9

(iii) Jules, 72, part-time computer games tester

11, 20, 9, 23, 13, 17, 18, 7, 9, 24

(b) Write about any differences you notice between Janet,
Linford and Jules.

F Writing a report

On the opposite page is a report on a project by some pupils
who wanted to find out if boys could run faster than girls.

The report says clearly what questions the pupils were asking.

It then describes how the data was collected.

It tells us about any problems which the pupils had to
overcome when collecting the data.

The data is recorded very clearly.

The report shows how the data is used to help answer
the question the pupils started with.

These pupils have decided to draw a dot plot to
illustrate the data.

They find the medians and the ranges to help them compare
the two sets of data.

At the end of the report the pupils state their conclusion,
based on the data they have collected.

Questions for discussion

- If you were doing this project, what other practical
  problems could arise? How would you solve them?
- Do you agree with the conclusion these pupils have drawn
  from their data? If not, what would your conclusion be?

Can boys in our class run faster than the girls?   by Andrew, Farnaaz and Leo

We wanted to know if the boys in our class can run faster then the girls.
We know Sean is the fastest boy because he got picked for the school team!

How we got our data

We got every person in our class to run from one end of the playground to the other, and we timed them with a stopwatch. We did it in some PE lessons.

We had to find the best way of timing. The way we did it was like this.
One person started the race by moving their arm down when they said "Go!"
The person at the other end moved their arm down when the runner crossed the line.
The person with the stopwatch was halfway along so that they could see easily.

Data

Boys' times (seconds)	9.3	11.2	12.2	10.0	9.5	13.4	12.2	11.7
	13.5	12.8	14.1	10.7	14.3	14.0		

Girls' times (seconds)	10.2	12.3	10.2	15.5	14.2	11.9	10.4	13.8
	13.3	9.9	12.1	11.7	13.4	10.8	13.5	10.2

Comparing the boys and girls

Dot plots of the boys' and girls' times

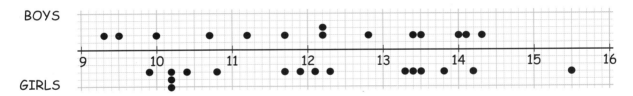

These diagrams show the medians, ranges and shortest and longest times.

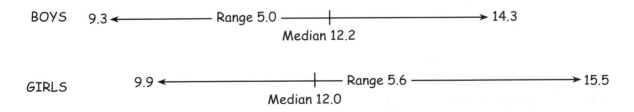

Conclusion

The two fastest runners were boys, the slowest was a girl.
Using the median for comparison, the girls were faster but only slightly.
The girls' times were a little more spread out than the boys'.

G Projects

Here are some ideas for projects that involve collecting data and making comparisons.

The Argon Factor   for the class working together

In the mental agility test you have one minute to memorise the shapes and numbers. 15 questions are then read out to you and you have 5 seconds to write down each answer. You will be scored out of 15.

In the memory test you have two minutes to remember the pictures and details of the four people. You then have 10 minutes to answer 20 questions on paper to see what you remember.

Start of the day and end of the day?   *Young people's memories and older people's?*

Handwriting size   for working in pairs or small groups

Ask a number of boys and a number of girls to write this sentence:

The quick brown fox jumps over the lazy dog.

Measure the length of the sentence in centimetres.

Compare the girls and the boys and write a report.

H Puzzles and problems

H1 Farina worked out the median and range of the ages of the seven people in her family.

One of the ages, and the median, got torn off.

What could they be?

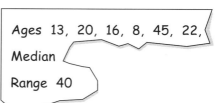

Ages 13, 20, 16, 8, 45, 22,

Median

Range 40

H2 There are seven trees in Paul's garden.
Their ages in years are 11, 15, 18, 20, 24, 25, 27

(a) What is the median age of the trees?

(b) One tree is chopped down.

Which tree could it be if the new median is

(i) 22   (ii) 21   (iii) 19

H3 (a) Brian and Cheryl carried out a survey of the number of people in cars going past their school.

They drew this pictogram.

1 person
2 people
3 people
4 people
5 people
6 people

What is the median number of people in a car?

(b) Later on they did another survey and recorded this data.
What is the median number of people in this case?

Number of people in car	1	2	3	4	5	6	7
Number of cars	20	17	13	16	9	2	1

*H4 Split this collection of numbers into two groups, so that one group consists of five numbers with median 55 and range 29, and the other group of four numbers with median 60 and range 31.

48	68	43
79	55	46
72	58	62

What progress have you made?

Statement

I can summarise a set of data using the median and range.

Evidence

1 Pat recorded his reaction times for each hand. The times in hundredths of a second were

Right hand
14, 12, 13, 17, 12, 14, 17, 14, 18, 12
Left hand
18, 9, 20, 16, 23, 8, 22, 24, 15

Find the median time, and the range of times, for each hand.

Compare the times for each hand.

I can carry out a project involving data collection and write a report on it.

Your project work and report should give evidence of this.

Fractions

This work will help you
◆ simplify fractions
◆ put fractions in order of size
◆ add and subtract fractions

A Equivalent fractions

This scale from 0 to 1 is divided into fifths and twentieths.

You can see that there are 4 twentieths in 1 fifth.

So you can change from fifths to twentieths by multiplying the numerator and denominator by 4.

To change twentieths to fifths, divide numerator and denominator by 4.

Going from $\frac{12}{20}$ to the equivalent fraction $\frac{3}{5}$ is called **simplifying**.
A fraction which cannot be simplified any more is in its **simplest form**.

A1 Copy these and fill in the missing numbers.

(a) $\frac{1}{8} = \frac{?}{16}$ (b) $\frac{4}{5} = \frac{?}{15}$ (c) $\frac{2}{3} = \frac{12}{?}$ (d) $\frac{3}{8} = \frac{12}{?}$

(e) $\frac{25}{40} = \frac{?}{8}$ (f) $\frac{16}{24} = \frac{2}{?}$ (g) $\frac{18}{30} = \frac{?}{10}$ (h) $\frac{45}{75} = \frac{3}{?}$

A2 There are three sets of equivalent fractions muddled up here.
Can you sort them out?

$\frac{9}{24}$ $\frac{8}{10}$ $\frac{2}{3}$ $\frac{3}{8}$ $\frac{4}{5}$ $\frac{10}{15}$ $\frac{16}{20}$ $\frac{8}{12}$ $\frac{6}{16}$

A3 Simplify each of these fractions as far as possible.

(a) $\frac{4}{6}$ (b) $\frac{6}{12}$ (c) $\frac{15}{20}$ (d) $\frac{8}{16}$ (e) $\frac{18}{21}$

(f) $\frac{18}{45}$ (g) $\frac{10}{35}$ (h) $\frac{16}{20}$ (i) $\frac{16}{24}$ (j) $\frac{12}{60}$

A4 Simplify each of these fractions as far as possible.
One of them cannot be simplified – which one?

(a) $\frac{4}{12}$ (b) $\frac{20}{45}$ (c) $\frac{30}{50}$ (d) $\frac{28}{42}$ (e) $\frac{18}{54}$

(f) $\frac{9}{16}$ (g) $\frac{24}{30}$ (h) $\frac{24}{32}$ (i) $\frac{15}{35}$ (j) $\frac{25}{60}$

A5 Write in its simplest form each of the fractions marked on the scale below.

(a)   (b)   (c)   (d)   (e)   (f)   (g)

A6 As a fraction, 0.15 is $\frac{15}{100}$.
Simplify $\frac{15}{100}$ as far as possible.

A7 Write each of these decimals as a fraction, in its simplest form.

(a) 0.24   (b) 0.06   (c) 0.95   (d) 0.33   (e) 0.32

(f) 0.8   (g) 0.45   (h) 0.12   (i) 0.85   (j) 0.02

A8 As a fraction, 0.165 is $\frac{165}{1000}$.
Write this fraction in its simplest form.

A9 Write each of these decimals as a fraction, as simply as possible.

(a) 0.275   (b) 0.125   (c) 0.148   (d) 0.055   (e) 0.008

A10 Each of these divisions is a hundredth.

The lower side of this scale is marked in twentieths.

What fractions are marked on the lower side of each of these sides?

twentieths

(a) ....ths

(b) ....ths

(c) ....ths

B Using equivalent fractions

Comparing fractions

It is easy to see that $\frac{3}{5}$ is greater than $\frac{2}{5}$, because the fractions have the same denominator.

It is not so easy to see whether $\frac{3}{5}$ is greater or less than $\frac{2}{3}$.

One way to compare them is to use equivalent fractions.

Fractions equal to $\frac{3}{5}$

$$\frac{3}{5} = \frac{6}{10} = \frac{9}{15} = \frac{12}{20} = \cdots$$
$$\uparrow$$

Fractions equal to $\frac{2}{3}$

$$\frac{2}{3} = \frac{4}{6} = \frac{6}{9} = \frac{8}{12} = \frac{10}{15} = \cdots$$
$$\uparrow$$

By changing $\frac{3}{5}$ and $\frac{2}{3}$ to denominator **15**, we see that $\frac{3}{5}$ is less than $\frac{2}{3}$.

B1 By using equivalent fractions, decide which is the larger fraction in each pair.

(a) $\frac{1}{3}, \frac{3}{8}$ (b) $\frac{2}{3}, \frac{5}{8}$ (c) $\frac{3}{4}, \frac{4}{5}$ (d) $\frac{3}{5}, \frac{5}{8}$

(e) $\frac{3}{7}, \frac{4}{9}$ (f) $\frac{3}{8}, \frac{4}{11}$ (g) $\frac{4}{7}, \frac{3}{5}$ (h) $\frac{4}{9}, \frac{9}{20}$

Mixed numbers

A **mixed number** consists of a whole number and a fraction, for example $2\frac{3}{4}$.

We can write $2\frac{3}{4}$ as a single fraction, but its numerator will be greater than its denominator (an **improper** fraction).

Because 1 is equivalent to $\frac{4}{4}$ it follows that $2 = \frac{8}{4}$.

So $2\frac{3}{4} = \frac{8}{4} + \frac{3}{4} = \frac{11}{4}$.

B2 Write each of these mixed numbers as an improper fraction.

(a) $1\frac{1}{3}$ (b) $2\frac{1}{4}$ (c) $3\frac{2}{5}$ (d) $1\frac{7}{10}$ (e) $2\frac{7}{8}$

B3 Write each of these improper fractions as a mixed number.

(a) $\frac{5}{2}$ (b) $\frac{5}{3}$ (c) $\frac{7}{4}$ (d) $\frac{11}{5}$ (e) $\frac{13}{5}$

Adding and subtracting fractions

It is easy to add $\frac{3}{5}$ and $\frac{1}{5}$ because the fractions have the same denominator.

It is not so easy to do $\frac{3}{5} + \frac{1}{3}$. We need to make the denominators the same.

We can change both fractions to denominator 15:

$$\frac{3}{5} = \frac{9}{15} \qquad \frac{1}{3} = \frac{5}{15} \qquad \text{So } \frac{3}{5} + \frac{1}{3} = \frac{9}{15} + \frac{5}{15} = \mathbf{\frac{14}{15}}$$

B4 Work these out.

(a) $\frac{1}{2} + \frac{1}{3}$ (b) $\frac{1}{3} + \frac{1}{4}$ (c) $\frac{1}{5} + \frac{1}{3}$ (d) $\frac{3}{8} + \frac{1}{4}$ (e) $\frac{2}{3} + \frac{1}{8}$

(f) $\frac{3}{8} + \frac{2}{5}$ (g) $\frac{3}{4} + \frac{5}{8}$ (h) $\frac{2}{3} + \frac{3}{4}$ (i) $\frac{5}{8} + \frac{1}{6}$ (j) $\frac{3}{4} + \frac{3}{10}$

B5 Work these out.

(a) $\frac{1}{2} - \frac{1}{3}$ (b) $\frac{1}{3} - \frac{1}{4}$ (c) $\frac{1}{3} - \frac{1}{5}$ (d) $\frac{5}{8} - \frac{1}{4}$ (e) $\frac{2}{3} - \frac{3}{8}$

(f) $\frac{5}{8} - \frac{2}{5}$ (g) $\frac{3}{5} - \frac{3}{8}$ (h) $\frac{3}{4} - \frac{2}{5}$ (i) $\frac{5}{8} - \frac{1}{6}$ (j) $\frac{5}{6} - \frac{3}{4}$

Multiplying a fraction by a whole number

$4 \times \frac{2}{3}$ means the same as $\frac{2}{3} + \frac{2}{3} + \frac{2}{3} + \frac{2}{3}$, which is $\frac{8}{3}$ or $2\frac{2}{3}$.

Similarly, $5 \times \frac{3}{4} = \frac{15}{4}$ or $3\frac{3}{4}$.

B6 Work these out.

(a) $6 \times \frac{2}{5}$ (b) $8 \times \frac{4}{5}$ (c) $\frac{3}{8} \times 10$ (d) $7 \times \frac{5}{6}$ (e) $4 \times \frac{5}{8}$

What progress have you made?

Statement	Evidence
I can simplify fractions.	1 Simplify these as far as possible. (a) $\frac{24}{30}$ (b) $\frac{27}{36}$
I can put fractions in order of size.	2 Which is larger, $\frac{5}{8}$ or $\frac{4}{7}$? Show your working.
I can change between mixed numbers and improper fractions.	3 (a) Change $2\frac{3}{5}$ to an improper fraction. (b) Change $\frac{28}{3}$ to a mixed number.
I can add and subtract fractions.	4 Work these out. (a) $\frac{3}{5} + \frac{1}{8}$ (b) $\frac{2}{3} - \frac{1}{4}$ (c) $\frac{5}{6} + \frac{3}{4}$
I can multiply a fraction by a whole number.	5 Work out (a) $6 \times \frac{7}{8}$ (b) $\frac{4}{5} \times 9$

⑩ Area

This work will help you
- ◆ find the area of a parallelogram
- ◆ find the area of a triangle
- ◆ find the area of a trapezium
- ◆ solve problems involving these shapes

A Area of a parallelogram

- This sketch shows a parallelogram.
  Draw the parallelogram accurately twice and cut out both shapes.
- Now cut one of them so you can make a rectangle from the pieces.
- What is the area of the parallelogram?

- Cut the other one to make a different rectangle.
- Does this give the same area as before?

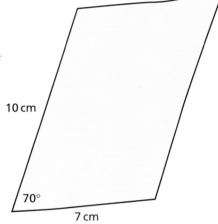

A1 Draw this parallelogram accurately.
By drawing or cutting show how to make it into a rectangle.
Find the area of the parallelogram.

A2 Find the area of this parallelogram in the same way as in A1.

Is there more than one way to make it into a rectangle?
Draw sketches of the different ways.

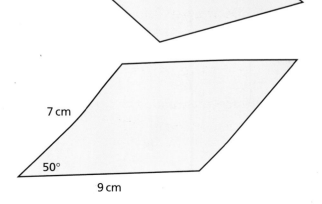

A3 This rectangle is split into two congruent right-angled triangles A and B with a parallelogram P between them.

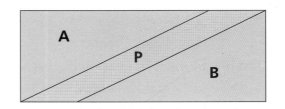

Triangle A slides along to touch triangle B. The original rectangle is now split into A, B and a rectangle R.

What can you say about the areas of P and R?

Explain the reason for your answer.

A4 Work out the area of each of these parallelograms. They are not drawn accurately.

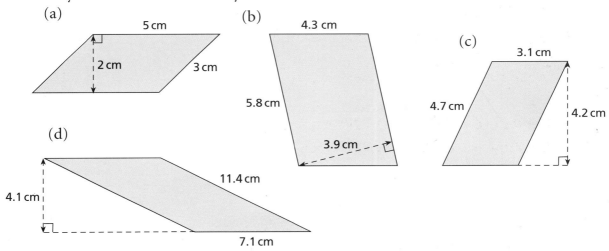

(a)
5 cm
2 cm
3 cm

(b)
4.3 cm
5.8 cm
3.9 cm

(c)
3.1 cm
4.7 cm
4.2 cm

(d)
11.4 cm
4.1 cm
7.1 cm

A5 Draw axes on squared paper. Label both axes from ⁻5 to 5.

(a) Draw a parallelogram with vertices at $(4, 0)$, $(4, 5)$, $(⁻2, 3)$ and $(⁻2, ⁻2)$. Calculate its area in square units.

(b) Draw a parallelogram with vertices at $(3, 4)$, $(⁻1, 4)$, $(⁻3, ⁻3)$ and $(1, ⁻3)$. Calculate its area.

(c) Calculate the area of the parallelogram with vertices at $(2, ⁻5)$, $(0, ⁻5)$, $(⁻5, 3)$ and $(⁻3, 3)$.

A6 This shape is made from two parallelograms. Calculate its area.

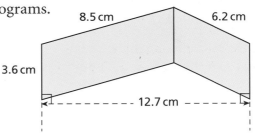

8.5 cm
6.2 cm
3.6 cm
12.7 cm

The rule for finding the area of a parallelogram can be written

area = base × height

The height must be measured at right angles to the base.

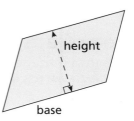

A7 Find the lengths marked with letters.
The diagrams are not drawn accurately.

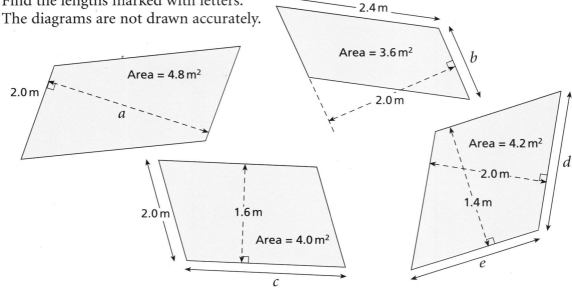

A8 Find the lengths marked with letters.
The diagrams are not drawn accurately.

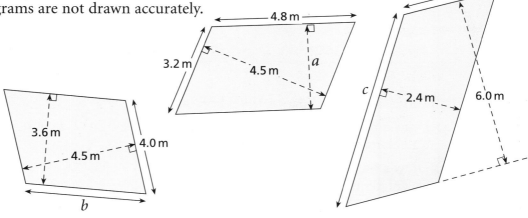

*A9 The vertices of a parallelogram are at
the points $(0, 0)$, $(5, 2)$, $(6, 6)$ and $(1, 4)$.

Without doing any measuring,
work out the area of the parallelogram,
in square units.

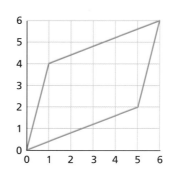

B Area of a triangle

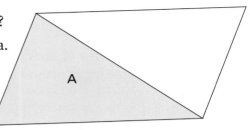

- What fraction of the parallelogram is triangle A?
- Measure the parallelogram and work out its area.
- What is the area of triangle A?
- Could you use a different parallelogram to work out the area of triangle A?

B1 Find the areas of the shaded triangles.

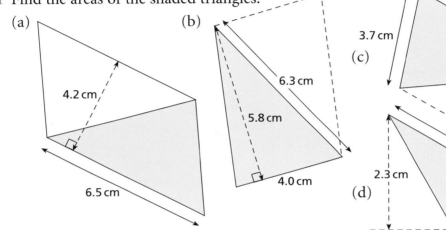

(a)

4.2 cm

6.5 cm

(b)

6.3 cm

5.8 cm

4.0 cm

(c)

6.0 cm

3.7 cm

3.4 cm

(d)

2.3 cm

4.1 cm

2.8 cm

B2 For each triangle,

- take measurements and record them on a sketch
- work out the area
- find the area using different measurements and check that you get the same result

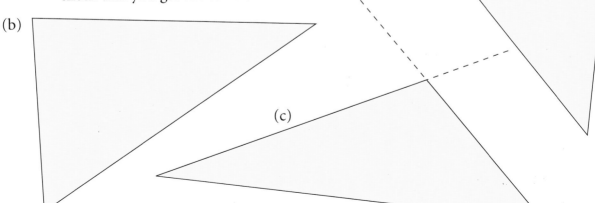

(a)

(b)

(c)

B3 Draw axes on squared paper and label them from ⁻5 to 5.
Draw a triangle with vertices at (⁻2, 2), (3, ⁻1) and (⁻2, ⁻3).
Calculate its area in square units.

B4 Calculate the area of each of these shapes.
They are not drawn accurately.

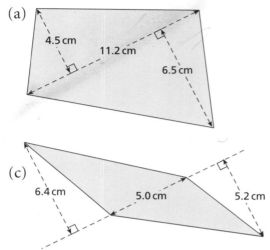

(a)
4.5 cm
11.2 cm
6.5 cm

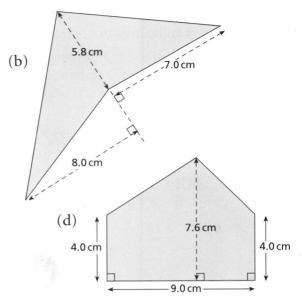

(b)
5.8 cm
7.0 cm
8.0 cm

(c)
6.4 cm
5.0 cm
5.2 cm

(d)
4.0 cm
7.6 cm
4.0 cm
9.0 cm

B5 Find the missing length in each of these.
They are not drawn accurately.

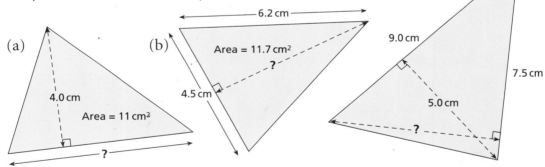

(a)
4.0 cm
Area = 11 cm²
?

(b)
6.2 cm
Area = 11.7 cm²
?
4.5 cm

(c)
9.0 cm
7.5 cm
5.0 cm
?

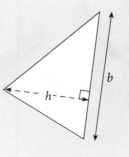

These formulas all say the same thing.

$$\text{Area of triangle} = \frac{\text{base} \times \text{height}}{2} \qquad A = \tfrac{1}{2}bh \qquad A = \frac{bh}{2}$$

Think of them as meaning

'work out base × height and halve it'.

Remember that b can be the length of any side of the triangle,
but h must be measured at right angles to b.

b
h

C Area of a trapezium

A trapezium is a quadrilateral with two parallel sides.

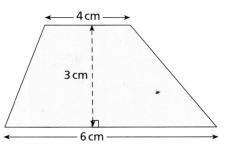

* How could you find the area of this trapezium?

C1 Work out the area of these trapeziums.
They are not drawn accurately.

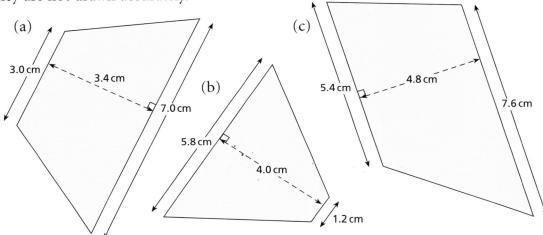

(a)
3.0 cm
3.4 cm
7.0 cm

(b)
5.8 cm
4.0 cm
1.2 cm

(c)
5.2 cm
5.4 cm
4.8 cm
7.6 cm

C2 Calculate the area of this trapezium.

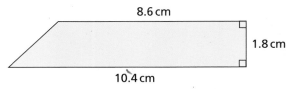

8.6 cm
1.8 cm
10.4 cm

C3 Measure each trapezium and work out its area.

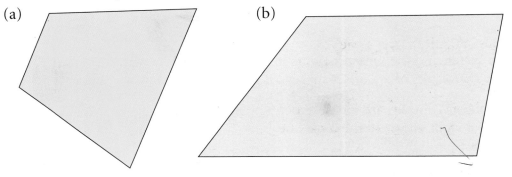

(a)

(b)

Splitting into two triangles gives this as a formula for the area of a trapezium:

$$A = \tfrac{1}{2}ah + \tfrac{1}{2}bh$$

But these are more usual ways of writing the formula:

$$A = \tfrac{1}{2}(a + b)h \qquad A = \frac{(a + b)h}{2}$$

You can think of them as saying

'add the lengths of the parallel sides, multiply by the distance between them, then halve'.

Remember that h must be measured at right angles to a and b.

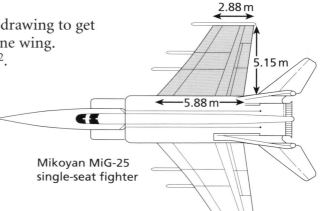

C4 Use the measurements shown on this drawing to get an estimate of the area of the top of one wing. Give your answer to the nearest 0.1 m².

Mikoyan MiG-25 single-seat fighter

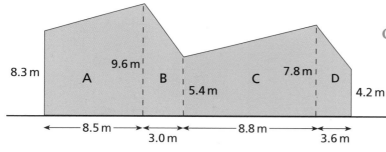

C5 (a) Work out the area of this factory wall.

(b) Work out the cost of heat insulation for this wall at £18.50 per square metre.

C6 This sketch and the measurements in metres show the results of an 'offset survey' of a field.

The offsets (dotted) are measurements made at right angles to the 'base line' ABCDEF.

Calculate the area of the field.

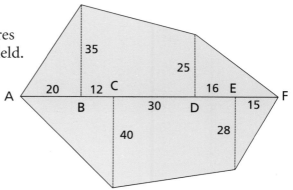

72

C7 The green area is a flower bed.
Its edges are two regular septagons with the same centre.

Work out the area of the flower bed.

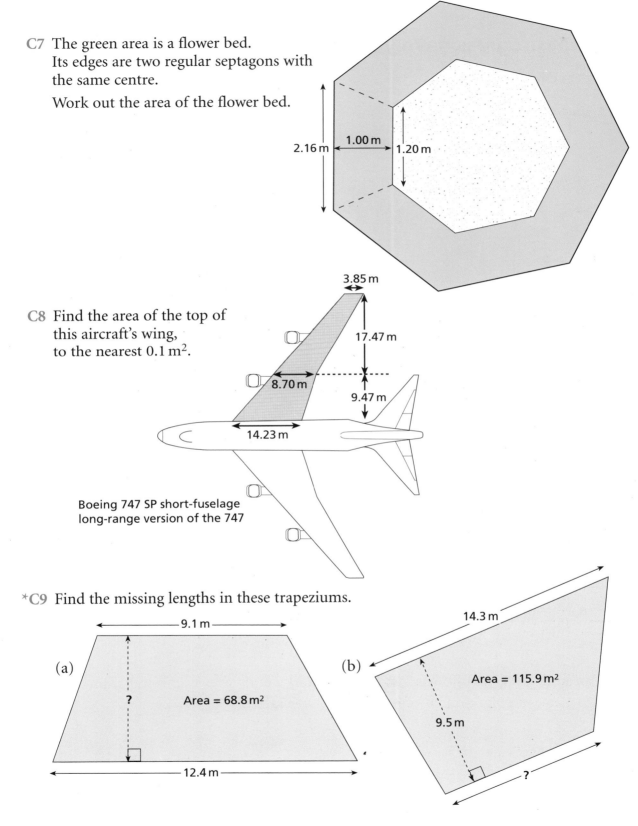

C8 Find the area of the top of this aircraft's wing, to the nearest 0.1 m².

Boeing 747 SP short-fuselage long-range version of the 747

*C9 Find the missing lengths in these trapeziums.

(a)

9.1 m

?

Area = 68.8 m²

12.4 m

(b)

14.3 m

Area = 115.9 m²

9.5 m

?

What progress have you made?

Statement   **Evidence**

I can work out areas of parallelograms.   1 Measure this parallelogram and
                                              work out its area.

2 Work out the area of this parallelogram.

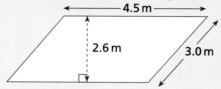

3 Work out the missing length.

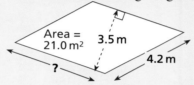

I can work out areas of triangles.   4 Measure this triangle and work out its area.

5 Work out the area of this triangle.

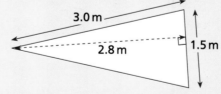

I can work out areas of trapeziums.   6 Work out the area of this trapezium.

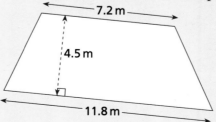

B1 (a) Copy and complete this arrow diagram.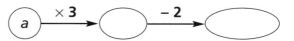

$a \xrightarrow{\times 3} \bigcirc \xrightarrow{-2} \bigcirc$

(b) Which of these shorthand rules is correct for the diagram?

| $a \to a - 6$ | $a \to 3(a - 2)$ | $a \to 3a - 2$ | $a \to 2(a - 3)$ | $a \to 2a - 3$ |

B2 Match each diagram to the correct rule.

Rules

(a) $c \xrightarrow{+4} \bigcirc \xrightarrow{\times 3} \bigcirc$

| $c \to c + 12$ | $c \to 3(c + 4)$ |
| $c \to 4c + 3$ | $c \to 4c \times 3$ |

(b) $p \xrightarrow{\times 2} \bigcirc \xrightarrow{+4} \bigcirc$

| $p \to 4p + 2$ | $p \to 2p + 4$ |
| $p \to p + 8$ | $p \to 2(p + 4)$ |

B3 Look at this shorthand rule: $s \to \frac{s}{4} + 5$.

Which of these diagrams is correct for the rule?

A $s \xrightarrow{\div 4} \bigcirc \xrightarrow{+5} \bigcirc$

B $s \xrightarrow{+5} \bigcirc \xrightarrow{\div 4} \bigcirc$

B4 Copy and complete these arrow diagrams.
For each of them, write a shorthand rule.

(a) $a \xrightarrow{\times 5} \bigcirc \xrightarrow{-3} \bigcirc$

(b) $a \xrightarrow{-3} \bigcirc \xrightarrow{\times 5} \bigcirc$

(c) $w \xrightarrow{+7} \bigcirc \xrightarrow{\div 2} \bigcirc$

(d) $w \xrightarrow{\div 2} \bigcirc \xrightarrow{+7} \bigcirc$

B5 Draw arrow diagrams for each of these rules.

(a) $s \to 4s + 5$ (b) $t \to \frac{t - 5}{3}$ (c) $w \to 5w - 7$
(d) $x \to \frac{x}{4} - 1$ (e) $y \to 7y + 3$ (f) $z \to 2(z + 5)$

B6 Complete this arrow diagram and write a shorthand rule for it.

$f \xrightarrow{\times 2} \bigcirc \xrightarrow{+3} \bigcirc \xrightarrow{\div 5} \bigcirc$

B7 This is Masood's homework. He has not done very well!
Do it correctly for him and explain what he has done wrong.

Complete each of these, and write down the rule.

(a) d —+ 10→ $d + 10$ —÷ 5→ $d + 2$

$d \rightarrow d + 2$ ✗

(b) s —+ 4→ $s + 4$ —× 3→ $s + 12$

$s \rightarrow s + 12$ ✗

(c) g —+ 4→ $g + 4$ —÷ 2→ $g + 2$

$g \rightarrow g + 2$ ✗

(d) a —− 10→ $a - 10$ —÷ 2→ $a - \dfrac{10}{2}$

$a \rightarrow a - 5$ ✗

(e) e —× 6→ $6e$ —− 2→ $4e$

$e \rightarrow 4e$ ✗

(f) h —÷ 4→ $\dfrac{h}{4}$ —− 2→ $\dfrac{h - 2}{4}$

$h \rightarrow \dfrac{h - 2}{4}$ ✗

C Evaluating expressions

Input		Output
p —× 5→ $5p$ —− 3→ $5p - 3$		

$p \rightarrow 5p - 3$
$3 \rightarrow 12$
$4 \rightarrow ?$

C1 Work out the value of $3a + 7$ when $a = 3$.

C2 Work out the value of $4(c - 5)$ when
   (a) $c = 7$ (b) $c = 10$ (c) $c = 20$ (d) $c = 5$

C3 For the rule $a \rightarrow \dfrac{a - 3}{2}$, copy and complete these.
   (a) $5 \rightarrow \ldots$ (b) $6 \rightarrow \ldots$ (c) $10 \rightarrow \ldots$

C4 Which number pairs in the box fit each of these rules?
   (a) $p \rightarrow p + 3$ (b) $r \rightarrow 5r - 1$ (c) $s \rightarrow 2(1 + s)$
   (d) $w \rightarrow 5 - w$ (e) $h \rightarrow 3h + 3$ (f) $k \rightarrow \dfrac{k}{2} + 3$

$1 \rightarrow 4$	$2 \rightarrow 9$
$3 \rightarrow 0$	$4 \rightarrow 5$
$5 \rightarrow 0$	$5 \rightarrow 12$

C5 Find three different shorthand rules which fit $4 \rightarrow 0$.

Cover up

Cut out the 8 cards on sheet 148.

Put the cards on the board so that each card covers two squares that fit the rule.

For example, $m \to m + 6$ may cover $4 \to 10$ and $6 \to 12$, or it may cover $6 \to 12$ and $0 \to 6$, and so on.

You can put the cards this way ☐ or this way ▯.

- 2, 3 or 4 cards on the board: very good.
- 5, 6 or 7 cards on the board: excellent.
- 8 cards on the board: brilliant!

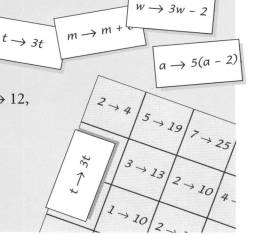

D Same but different!

Put three or four different numbers for **a** through this arrow diagram.

What do you notice?

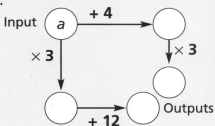

What must **?** be to get a similar result?

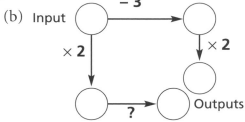

D1 Find what you have to replace **?** by so that, whatever the input is, the two outputs are the same.

(a)
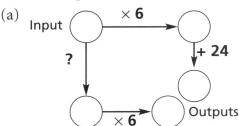

(b)
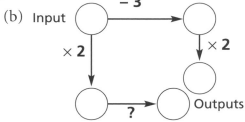

(c)
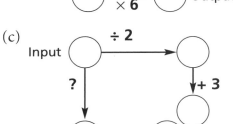

(d)
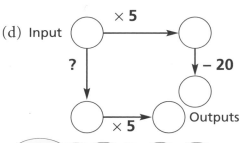

Write about anything you notice.

81

E Equivalent expressions

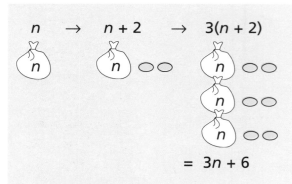

$$n \rightarrow n + 2 \rightarrow 3(n + 2)$$

$$= 3n + 6$$

$3(n + 2)$ and $3n + 6$ are
equivalent expressions.

They have the same value,
whatever the value of n.

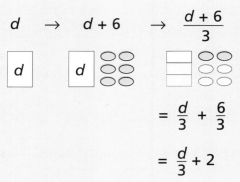

$$d \rightarrow d + 6 \rightarrow \frac{d + 6}{3}$$

$$= \frac{d}{3} + \frac{6}{3}$$

$$= \frac{d}{3} + 2$$

$\frac{d + 6}{3}$ and $\frac{d}{3} + 2$ are
equivalent expressions.

E1 Copy and complete these.

(a) $2a + 8 = \heartsuit(a + 4)$

(b) $4a - 12 = 4(a - \blacktriangle)$

(c) $\dfrac{a - 6}{2} = \dfrac{a}{2} - \bullet$

(d) $5a - 20 = \blacksquare(a - \blacklozenge)$

(e) $\dfrac{a + \blacktriangledown}{3} = \dfrac{a}{\blacklozenge} + 12$

(f) $\heartsuit a + 6 = 3(a + \blacklozenge)$

E2 There are three pairs of equivalent expressions here.
Pair them up, and find the odd one left over.

$3x + 18$ $3(x - 2)$ $3x - 6$ $3(x + 6)$ $3x - 18$ $3(x - 6)$ $3x - 2$

E3 Find an equivalent expression for each of these:

(a) $3(x - a)$

(b) $\dfrac{b + 10}{2}$

(c) $5(c - 30)$

(d) $4(d - 2)$

(e) $0.5(e + 6)$

(f) $8(w + \frac{1}{2})$

(g) $\dfrac{a + 20}{5}$

(h) $70(m - 0.1)$

(i) $6(2 + f)$

(j) $3(9 + y)$

(k) $\dfrac{6 + k}{2}$

(l) $1.5(n + 20)$

E4 Copy and complete each arrow diagram and match it with two shorthand rules from the box.

Check your answers by putting $a = 3$ and $a = 5$ in each diagram and its rules.

(a) a —$\times$ **3**→ ◯ —$-$ **2**→ ◯ —$\times$ **4**→ ◯

(b) a —$\times$ **2**→ ◯ —$-$ **4**→ ◯ —$\times$ **3**→ ◯

(c) a —$\times$ **4**→ ◯ —$-$ **3**→ ◯ —$\times$ **2**→ ◯

$a \to 3(2a - 4)$
$a \to 6a - 12$
$a \to 4(3a - 2)$
$a \to 8a - 6$
$a \to 2(4a - 3)$
$a \to 12a - 8$

E5 (a) Copy and complete this working for the expression $2(3a + 5)$.

(b) Write down an equivalent expression to $2(3a + 5)$.

$2(3a + 5)$
$= 2 \times (3a + 5)$
$= 2 \times 3a + 2 \times \bullet$
$= \bullet a + \bullet$

E6 Find an equivalent expression for each of these.

(a) $2(4x + 1)$ (b) $4(3 + 5y)$ (c) $3(2z - 3)$ (d) $5(6 + 3w)$ (e) $2(8 - 2u)$

(f) $\dfrac{2v + 12}{2}$ (g) $\dfrac{8 + 10t}{2}$ (h) $\dfrac{15s - 20}{5}$ (i) $\dfrac{24 + 3r}{2}$ (j) $\dfrac{18 - 2q}{6}$

E7 Copy and complete each of these.

(a) $3(2a + 3) = \blacksquare a + 9$

(b) $4(4c + \blacklozenge) = \heartsuit c + 12$

(c) $5(\heartsuit e + \blacktriangle) = 15e + 30$

(d) $\bullet(\blacklozenge d + 7) = 6d + 21$

(e) $\dfrac{12e + \blacktriangle}{\bullet} = 3e + 2$

(f) $\dfrac{8g + 24}{\blacklozenge} = g + \blacktriangledown$

Expression snap   a game for two or more players

Each player needs a set of 'Expression snap' cards on sheet 149.

Players take it in turns to turn over one of their cards on to their pile.

If the card turned over is equivalent to one on top of another pile, the first player to say 'SNAP' takes all the cards in the matching piles.

A wrong 'snap' means you lose the cards in your pile.

The first player to run out of cards loses.

F Inventing puzzles

Think of a number.

Multiply it by 2.

Add on 6.

Divide by 2.

Take off the number
you first thought of.

What is your answer?

Think of a number.

Add on 5.

Multiply it by 4.

Subtract 8.

Divide by 2.

Add 2.

Divide by 2.

Take off the number
you first thought of.

What is your answer?

F1 Try some different starting numbers
for this puzzle.

What answer do you always get?

Write an algebraic explanation for the puzzle.

> Think of a number.
> - Multiply it by 4.
> - Add on 20.
> - Divide by 4.
> - Take off your first number.
>
> What is your answer?

F2 Try some different starting numbers
for this puzzle.

What do you notice about the answers?

Write an algebraic explanation.

> Think of a number.
> - Multiply it by 2.
> - Add on 10.
> - Divide by 2.
> - Take off 5.
>
> What is your answer?

F3 What do you notice about the answers for these?
Write an algebraic explanation.

(a)
> Think of a number.
> - Add on 5.
> - Multiply it by 4.
> - Subtract 20.
> - Divide by 4.
> - Take off your first number.
>
> What is your answer?

(b)
> Think of a number.
> - Add on 3.
> - Multiply it by 2.
> - Subtract 6.
> - Divide by 2.
> - Add 2.
> - Take off your first number.
>
> What is your answer?

F4 Use algebra to explain each of these

(a)
> Think of a number.
> - Subtract 2.
> - Multiply it by 3.
> - Add 14.
> - Add your first number.
> - Divide by 4.
> - Take off your first number.
>
> What is your answer?

(b)
> Think of a number.
> - Subtract 4.
> - Multiply it by 5.
> - Add 20.
> - Take off your first number.
> - Divide by 4.
>
> What is your answer?

F5 Write a puzzle for this algebraic explanation!

> Think of a number.
> ....
> ....
> ....
> ....
> The answer is always 9.

x
2x
2x + 18
x + 9
9

F6 Work out the missing number (?) in this puzzle so that the answer is always 8.

> Think of a number.
> Multiply it by 2.
> Add on ?
> Divide by 2.
> Take off your first number.
> The answer is always 8.

F7 Explain this puzzle using algebra.

> Think of a number. Multiply it by 3.
> Add 15. Divide by 3. Take off 5.
> The answer is the number you first thought of.

F8 Invent a puzzle of your own where the answer is always 10. Write an algebraic explanation.

F9 Invent a puzzle of your own where the answer is always the number you first thought of. Write an algebraic explanation.

F10 Look at this diagram.
The top and bottom rules are the same,
and the side rules are the same.

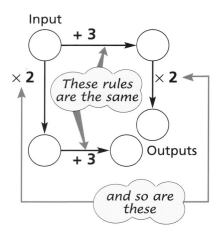

(a) Input any number.
What are the output numbers?

(b) Try some different input numbers.
What do you notice about
the difference in the outputs?

(c) Use algebra to explain what you notice.

(d) What happens if (i) you change the + 3 rule
(ii) you change the × 2 rule

Write about what you notice, and explain it.

What progress have you made?

Statement	Evidence

I can use shorthand rules.

1 Draw an arrow diagram for
(a) $y \to 3y - 6$ (b) $x \to \dfrac{x + 4}{2}$

2 If $m = 5$ work out the value of these.
(a) $3m + 4$ (b) $\dfrac{m + 20}{2}$ (c) $\dfrac{m}{2} - 1$

**I can work with equivalent
expressions.**

3 Find equivalent expressions to these.
(a) $4(x - 3)$ (b) $15s + 10$ (c) $\dfrac{h + 12}{2}$
(d) $3(2y - 5)$ (e) $6(5z + 1)$ (f) $\dfrac{8e + 4}{2}$

I can use algebra to explain puzzles.

4 Use algebra to explain why this puzzle
always gives the same number.

> Think of a number.
> Multiply it by 5.
> Add 50.
> Divide by 5.
> Take off 3.
> Take off the number you thought of.
> What is your answer?

⑫ Decimals

This is about calculation and approximation.
The work will help you

- ◆ multiply and divide decimals mentally and on paper
- ◆ round numbers and estimate the result of a calculation

A Multiplying and dividing by 10, 100, 0.1, …

Multiplying by 10 moves every digit one place to the left.
Dividing by 10 moves every digit one place to the right.

$$0.47 \xrightarrow{\times 10} 4.7 \qquad 4.7 \xrightarrow{\div 10} 0.47$$

Multiplying by 100 moves every digit two places to the left.
Dividing by 100 moves every digit two places to the right.

$$0.083 \xrightarrow{\times 100} 8.3 \qquad 8.3 \xrightarrow{\div 100} 0.083$$

Similarly for multiplication and division by 1000, 10 000, etc.

Multiplying by 0.1 is the same as dividing by 10.
So dividing by 0.1 is the same as multiplying by 10.

$$4.7 \xrightarrow{\times 0.1} 0.47 \qquad 0.47 \xrightarrow{\div 0.1} 4.7$$

Multiplying by 0.01 is the same as dividing by 100,
so dividing by 0.01 is the same as multiplying by 100.

$$8.3 \xrightarrow{\times 0.01} 0.083 \qquad 0.083 \xrightarrow{\div 0.01} 8.3$$

Similarly for multiplication and division by 0.001, 0.0001, etc.

A1 Work these out.

   (a) 0.065×100 (b) $36.78 \div 100$ (c) $274.3 \div 1000$ (d) 1000×0.012

   (e) 10×0.084 (f) $33.7 \div 1000$ (g) $0.005\,46 \times 1000$ (h) $0.308 \div 100$

   (i) $10\,000 \times 0.0501$ (j) $0.898 \div 1000$ (k) $2.62 \div 100$ (l) $1000 \times 0.002\,37$

A2 Convert

   (a) 2.3 km to metres   (b) 0.037 kg to grams   (c) 17.3 m to kilometres

   (d) 2080 ml to litres   (e) 0.977 cm to metres   (f) 23.04 m to kilometres

A3 Work these out.

   (a) 0.865×0.1 (b) $36.78 \div 0.1$ (c) 224.3×0.01 (d) 56.9×0.001

   (e) 0.1×0.064 (f) $28.7 \div 0.1$ (g) 536×0.001 (h) $708 \div 0.01$

A4 Convert

(a) 2.3 mm to metres   (b) 0.0075 kg to grams   (c) 0.032 km to centimetres

(d) 0.0503 litres to ml   (e) 3.05 cm to metres   (f) 0.0955 m to millimetres

A5 What number is missing in each of these?

(a) $4.26 \times ? = 0.0426$ (b) $4.26 \div ? = 0.0426$ (c) $87.3 \div ? = 873$

(d) $0.0618 \times ? = 61.8$ (e) $3.71 \div ? = 371$ (f) $402.6 \div ? = 0.4026$

A6 Arrange these cards to make three correct calculations.

0.02375	2.375	0.002375	× 0.001 =	23750	÷ 0.1 =
	× 0.01 =		23.75		237.5

237.5

B From 3×2 to 30×200, 0.3×0.2, …

The multiplications 30×20, 30×0.02 and 0.03×2000 are all related to 3×2.

Here is a way of getting from 3×2 to 30×20.

$3 \times 2 = 6$
$\rightarrow \quad 30 \times 2 = 60$
$\rightarrow \quad 30 \times 20 = 600$

Explain how each line follows from the one above it.

Here is a way of getting from 3×2 to 30×0.02.

$3 \times 2 = 6$
$\rightarrow \quad 30 \times 2 = 60$
$\rightarrow \quad 30 \times 0.2 = 6$
$\rightarrow \quad 30 \times 0.02 = 0.6$

Explain how each line follows from the one above it.

B1 Work these out without a calculator.

(a) 30×200 (b) 300×200 (c) 0.3×20 (d) 0.3×200 (e) 0.3×0.2

(f) 50×40 (g) 500×4000 (h) 0.5×400 (i) 0.5×4 (j) 0.05×400

B2 Work these out without a calculator.

(a) 0.6×0.3 (b) 0.4×0.3 (c) 200×0.9 (d) 500×0.06 (e) 20×0.08

B3 Here is a set of numbers. From this set, find as many pairs as possible whose product is

| 0.05 | 0.5 | 5 | 50 | 500 |
| 0.06 | 0.6 | 6 | 60 | 600 |

   (a) 30   (b) 3   (c) 300

   (d) 25   (e) 2.5   (f) 0.36

B4 (a) What is the total length, in metres, of 40 plastic tubes, each 80 cm long?

   (b) How many 20 cm strips can be cut from 100 metres?

   (c) How many 60 ml bottles can be filled from 3 litres?

   (d) How many paces each 80 cm long have a total length of 400 metres?

   (e) How many pieces, each weighing 20 g, can be cut from 2.4 kg?

B5 The number 50 is fed into this chain of number machines.

   (a) What is the output?

   (b) What is the output if the machines are arranged in this order?

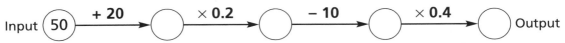

   (c) What is the largest output you can get by changing the order of the machines? (The starting number is still 50.)

B6 The number 40 is fed into this chain of number machines.

   What is the largest output you can get by changing the order of the machines?

B7 Arrange these cards to make three correct multiplications.

B8 Arrange these cards to make four correct multiplications.

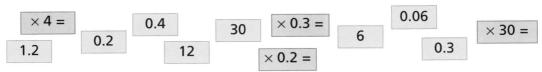

C Rounding to one significant figure

A book gives the population of a town as 58 357. The figure which has the highest value in this number is the **ten thousands** figure. It is called the **most significant figure**.

If we round 58 357 to the nearest ten thousand, we get **60 000**.

This is called rounding it to **one significant figure** (1 s.f.).

58357 ──── rounded to 1 s.f. ───→ **60000**

↑
most significant figure
(ten thousands)

C1 Which is the most significant figure in the number 4293?

Round 4293 to one significant figure.

C2 Round each of these to 1 s.f.

(a) 3571　　(b) 8294　　(c) 24 841　　(d) 752　　(e) 836 472　　(f) 39 457

In the number 0.043 15, the 4 has the highest value. It is in the second decimal place.

To round 0.043 15 to one significant figure, we round it to two decimal places and get **0.04**.

0.04315 ──── rounded to 1 s.f. ───→ **0.04**

↑
most significant figure

C3 Round to 1 s.f.　(a) 0.278　　(b) 0.053 17　　(c) 0.002 673 1　(d) 0.000 553

How to round to one significant figure

Look along the number from left to right. The first, or most, significant figure is the first non-zero figure you come to.

If the next figure is 5 or more, round up. Otherwise round down.

76056 ──────→ **80000**

0.00316584 ──────→ **0.003**

C4 Round to 1 s.f.　(a) 0.0682　　(b) 132 780　　(c) 88 302　　(d) 0.007 021

C5 Round to 1 s.f.　(a) 50.682　　(b) 1.572　　(c) 0.000 813　　(d) 0.0751

D Estimation

You can get a rough estimate of the result of a multiplication, by rounding the numbers to 1 s.f.

426 × 58 is roughly 400 × 60

which is

24 000

D1 Estimate these by rounding the numbers to 1 s.f.

Then use a calculator to find the correct answer and check that your estimate was reasonably close.

(a) 31×77 (b) 416×28 (c) 387×210

(d) 217×3958 (e) 4963×433 (f) 1835×293

D2 Estimate these by rounding the numbers to 1 s.f.

Check with a calculator as before.

(a) 67.71×9.17 (b) 0.4837×2.147 (c) 0.0236×47.59

(d) 0.7743×0.2079 (e) 5.638×0.0248

D3 These calculations are wrong.
The decimal point in the answer is in the wrong place.

Without using a calculator, write down the correct answers.

(a) $5.78 \times 0.18 = 10.404$ (b) $361 \times 0.0412 = 1.48732$

(c) $0.763 \times 0.127 = 0.96901$ (d) $45.38 \times 0.00682 = 0.03094916$

D4 There are 2.54 centimetres in an inch, 12 inches in a foot and 5280 feet in a mile. Estimate roughly the number of centimetres in a mile.

D5 A classroom is 18.63 metres long, 7.35 metres wide and 3.18 metres high. Estimate its volume in cubic metres.

D6 Estimate these by rounding the numbers to 1 s.f.

Then use a calculator and check that your estimate was close.

(a) $\dfrac{782.6 \times 0.096}{2.14}$ (b) $\dfrac{0.541 \times 58.38}{11.3}$ (c) $\dfrac{0.0772 \times 18.34}{4.174}$

(d) $\dfrac{238.2}{3.66 \times 5.31}$ (e) $\dfrac{5794}{61.3 \times 0.52}$ (f) $\dfrac{915.8}{0.926 \times 48.7}$

E Written multiplication

23.4×0.06 First get a rough idea of the answer, by rounding: $20 \times 0.06 = 1.2$

Ignore the decimal points. Multiply 234 by 6.

$$\begin{array}{r} 234 \\ \times \quad 6 \\ \hline 1404 \end{array}$$

Decide where to put the decimal point in the result:

$$23.4 \times 0.06 = \mathbf{1.404}$$

12.6×400 First get a rough idea of the answer, by rounding: $10 \times 400 = 4000$

Multiply 126 by 4.

$$\begin{array}{r} 126 \\ \times \quad 4 \\ \hline 504 \end{array}$$

Adjust the result: $12.6 \times 400 = \mathbf{5040}$

E1 Work these out.

(a) 42×0.8 (b) 0.7×2.7 (c) 0.8×26 (d) 0.13×0.6

(e) 9.2×0.06 (f) 500×0.88 (g) 2.6×0.004 (h) 7.83×0.3

E2 You are told that $156 \times 8 = 1248$.
Write down the answer to each of these.

(a) 1.56×8 (b) 15.6×0.8 (c) 0.156×800 (d) 1.56×0.08

E3 You are told that $1327 \times 4 = 5308$.
Write down the answer to each of these.

(a) 132.7×0.4 (b) 13.27×0.04 (c) 0.1327×400 (d) 132.7×0.004

F Dividing by a decimal

Sometimes you may need to divide by a decimal.
You can often change it to a whole number by multiplying
'top and bottom' by 10 or 100.

$$8 \div 0.2 = \frac{8}{0.2} \xrightarrow{\times 10} = \frac{80}{2} = \mathbf{40} \qquad 1.5 \div 0.03 = \frac{1.5}{0.03} \xrightarrow{\times 100} = \frac{150}{3} = \mathbf{50}$$

F1 (a) $\dfrac{6}{0.3}$ (b) $\dfrac{12}{0.2}$ (c) $\dfrac{30}{0.5}$ (d) $18 \div 0.6$ (e) $2.4 \div 0.3$

F2 (a) $\dfrac{1.4}{0.2}$ (b) $\dfrac{0.32}{0.8}$ (c) $\dfrac{0.18}{0.3}$ (d) $\dfrac{0.06}{0.3}$ (e) $\dfrac{120}{0.4}$

F3 (a) $\dfrac{1.2}{0.03}$ (b) $\dfrac{2.8}{0.04}$ (c) $\dfrac{16}{0.08}$ (d) $\dfrac{0.8}{0.02}$ (e) $\dfrac{8}{0.04}$

(f) $0.6 \div 0.3$ (g) $4 \div 0.05$ (h) $0.15 \div 0.03$ (i) $3 \div 0.06$ (j) $28 \div 0.07$

F4 Arrange these cards to make four correct calculations.

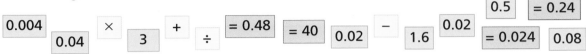

G Written division

Examples

$\dfrac{58.8}{300}$ Divide top and bottom by 100: $\dfrac{58.8}{300} = \dfrac{0.588}{3}$ $3\overline{)0.588}$ = 0.196

$\dfrac{62.4}{0.04}$ Get rid of decimals on the bottom.
Here we multiply top and bottom by 100: $\dfrac{62.4}{0.04} = \dfrac{6240}{4}$ $4\overline{)6240}$ = 1560

G1 Work these out.

(a) $\dfrac{32.2}{40}$ (b) $\dfrac{7.92}{0.2}$ (c) $\dfrac{2.24}{0.05}$ (d) $\dfrac{6.48}{900}$ (e) $\dfrac{11.2}{0.07}$

(f) $\dfrac{44.1}{0.06}$ (g) $\dfrac{1.68}{0.03}$ (h) $\dfrac{5.2}{50}$ (i) $\dfrac{0.54}{0.8}$ (j) $\dfrac{34.2}{0.04}$

G2 You are told that $\dfrac{2412}{4} = 603$. Write down the answer to each of these.

(a) $\dfrac{2.412}{0.4}$ (b) $\dfrac{241.2}{0.4}$ (c) $\dfrac{24.12}{40}$ (d) $\dfrac{0.2412}{400}$ (e) $\dfrac{241.2}{0.04}$

G3 You are told that $346 \times 8 = 2768$. Write down the answer to each of these.

(a) $\dfrac{2768}{8}$ (b) $\dfrac{27.68}{0.08}$ (c) $\dfrac{2.768}{800}$ (d) $\dfrac{276.8}{0.08}$ (e) $\dfrac{0.2768}{0.008}$

G4 Use the fact that $\dfrac{241}{4} = 60.25$ to write down the answer to

(a) $\dfrac{2.41}{0.4}$ (b) $\dfrac{0.0241}{0.004}$ (c) $\dfrac{0.241}{40}$ (d) $\dfrac{24.1}{400}$ (e) $\dfrac{24\,100}{0.04}$

93

H Rounding to two or more significant figures

<table>
<tr><td colspan="2">How to round to two significant figures</td></tr>
<tr><td>Identify the first significant figure. The next figure, whatever it is, is the second significant figure.</td><td>If the third significant figure is 5 or more, round the second figure up. Otherwise round down.</td></tr>
</table>

$$76\text{\small 056} \longrightarrow 76000$$
$$0.0030\text{\small 6584} \longrightarrow 0.0031$$

H1 Round each of these numbers to 2 s.f.

(a) 67 325   (b) 0.067 34   (c) 0.147 48   (d) 459.62   (e) 0.003 67

(f) 0.731 67   (g) 78.5202   (h) 901.32   (i) 50 865.5   (j) 1007.54

H2 Round each of these numbers to 3 s.f.

(a) 78 301   (b) 0.173 39   (c) 2001.48   (d) 3712.6   (e) 0.005 57

(f) 0.001 543   (g) 1278.66   (h) 903.135   (i) 850.54   (j) 49 871.2

H3 (a) Round 574.631 to 1 s.f.   (b) Round 574.631 to 2 s.f.

      (c) Round 574.631 to 3 s.f.   (d) Round 574.631 to 4 s.f.

I Different ways of rounding

There are two different ways of rounding numbers.

We can round to the nearest hundred, nearest tenth (or one decimal place), and so on.

Examples

73 426 to the nearest hundred is 73 400

4.587 to the nearest tenth (or to one decimal place) is 4.6

We can round to one significant figure, two significant figures, and so on.

Examples

73 426 to two significant figures is 73 000

4.587 to three significant figures is 4.59

I1 Round 5.326 to   (a) two decimal places   (b) two significant figures

I2 Round 3571 to   (a) the nearest hundred   (b) one significant figure

I3 Match each instruction on the left with a number on the right.

(a) Round 6.5674 to 1 d.p.   (b) Round 6.518 23 to 2 d.p.

(c) Round 0.007 821 3 to 3 d.p.   (d) Round 0.008 910 5 to 1 s.f.

(e) Round 6.521 to 2 s.f.   (f) Round 0.007 817 23 to 3 s.f.

6.5	0.007 82
6.52	0.009
6.6	0.008

I4 Round   (a) 3462 to the nearest ten   (b) 3462 to 1 s.f.

(c) 46 708 to 3 s.f.   (d) 46 708 to the nearest thousand

(e) 7.438 61 to 2 d.p.   (f) 7.438 61 to 2 s.f.

I5 Round   (a) 20.037 to 2 s.f.   (b) 20.037 to 2 d.p.

(c) 0.005 891 to 3 d.p.   (d) 0.005 891 to 3 s.f.

(e) 5.098 21 to 3 d.p.   (f) 5.098 21 to 3 s.f.

What progress have you made?

Statement	Evidence
I can work out multiplications like 300×0.04 without using a calculator.	1 Without using a calculator, work these out and show your working. (a) 300×0.04 (b) 0.4×0.2 (c) 7000×0.004
I can round to a given number of significant figures.	2 (a) Round 78 457 to 1 s.f. (b) Round 0.027 46 to 2 s.f. (c) Round 375.622 to 2 s.f. (d) Round 7.396 25 to 3 s.f.
I can estimate the result of a calculation by rounding to one significant figure.	3 Estimate the results of these calculations by rounding the numbers to 1 s.f. (a) 68.42×0.539 (b) $0.037 31 \times 286.56$ (c) $\dfrac{785.419 \times 0.2248}{39.375}$
I can do multiplications like 3.4×0.73 without a calculator.	4 Work out (a) 3.4×0.73 (b) 0.68×0.14
I can do divisions like $180 \div 0.6$ without a calculator.	5 Work out (a) $180 \div 0.6$ (b) $4.5 \div 0.05$
I can do divisions like $12.88 \div 2.3$ without a calculator.	6 Work out (a) $12.88 \div 2.3$ (b) $9.72 \div 0.36$

⑬ Investigations

This work is about investigating mathematics for yourself.

A Crossing points

On the opposite page is Chris's report on an investigation.

Say what the investigation is about.

First Chris tells us what the investigation is about.

Say what you do.
Be systematic.

Then she tells us how she is going to start.
She is going to be **systematic**.

What does this mean?

Show your working.
Say what you find out.

Next she tells us what she found out.

State any decisions you make.

Chris tells us about a decision she makes.

Why do you think she decided to concentrate on the maximum number?

Write your results in a table.

She makes a table of her results.
This will make it easier to spot any patterns.

Can you see any pattern in these numbers?

Crossing points

Report by Chris Sparrow, 8T

I am investigating how many crossing points there are with different numbers of straight lines.

I am going to start with 2 lines, then 3, then 4 and so on, and see how many crossing points I get.

Then I am going to see if there is a pattern in the numbers.

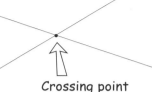

Crossing point

2 lines

With 2 lines you get 1 crossing point, or none if the lines are parallel.

3 lines

With 3 lines you can get 0, 1, 2 or 3 crossing points.

From now on I am going to find the <u>maximum</u> number of crossing points.

4 lines

5 lines

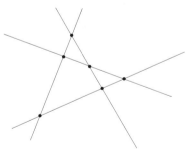

6 crossing points

10 crossing points

Number of lines			2	3	4	5
Maximum number of crossing points			1	3	6	10

Write about any patterns you see.

Chris notices a pattern in the table and writes about it.

Make a prediction ...

She makes a prediction ...

... and check it.

... and goes on to check it.

Write about anything interesting you notice.

She notices something interesting and writes about it.

Summarise your findings. Explain them if you can.

Chris tells us her main conclusion.

Chris has not tried to explain why her rule is true. Can you explain why it is true?

If possible, extend your investigation.

She is going to extend her investigation.

Carry out this further investigation yourself.

Number of lines	2	3	4	5
Maximum number of crossing points	1	3	6	10

+ 2   + 3   + 4

I have noticed that the gap between these numbers goes up by 1 each time.

I predict that with 6 lines there will be 15 crossing points.

6 lines

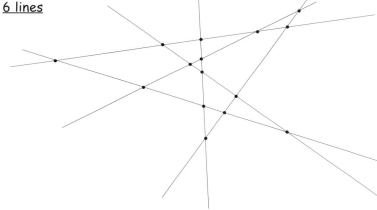

There are 15 crossing points, as predicted.

I have also noticed that each line has 5 crossing points on it.
When there were 5 lines, each one had 4 crossing points on it, and so on.

As you increase the number of lines, the maximum number of crossing points goes up by 1 more each time.

I am going to investigate the number of closed spaces you get.

1   2
3

B Some ideas

B1 Round table

Five people sit at a round table.

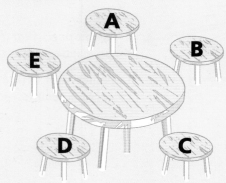

- Arrange them round the table in a different way so that nobody sits next to a person they sat next to before.
- How many ways can they be arranged like this?
- Investigate for different numbers of people.

B2 Nine lines

Nine straight lines can be drawn so they form different numbers of squares.

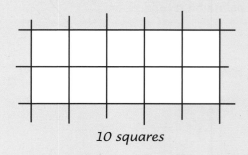

10 squares

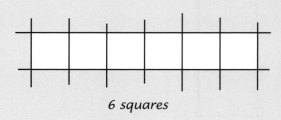

6 squares

- What other number of squares can you make with nine lines?
- Investigate for other numbers of lines.

B3 Cutting a cake

Sam has a square cake and
a long straight knife.

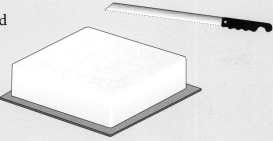

With three cuts, he cuts
the cake into 5 pieces.

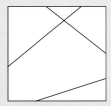

- What other numbers of pieces can you make with three cuts?
- Investigate for different numbers of cuts.

B4 Matchstick networks

Networks can be made by
joining matchsticks end to end.

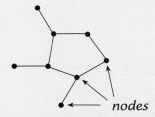

Points where matchsticks meet or end are called **nodes.**

Some networks
have enclosed spaces.

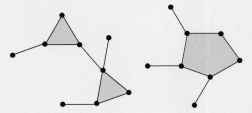

- Draw some matchstick networks.
- For each network, count
  - (i) the number of enclosed spaces
  - (ii) the number of nodes
  - (iii) the number of matchsticks

Are there any connections?
Investigate.

B5 Turn, turn, turn

To make a turning track

- Choose a set of whole numbers.
  (These tell you how far to move forward each time.)
- Decide if you are going to turn right or left after each move.
- Mark your starting position.

This track repeats the numbers 1, 2, 4 and turns right after each move.

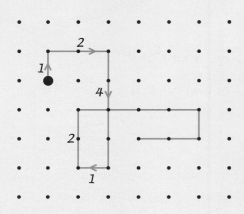

You must keep going, using your numbers in order.
Always make a 90° turn after each move.

- Copy and continue the turning track above.
  Describe what happens.
- Investigate tracks made with different sets of three numbers.
- What happens if you try sets of two numbers? four numbers? and so on …

⑭ Parallel lines

This is about parallel lines.
The work will help you

◆ draw and find parallel lines
◆ work with angles and parallel lines

A Using parallel lines

If you slide a line without turning it …

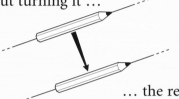

… the result is a line **parallel** to the first line.

Parallel lines go in the same direction, or have the same slope.
They don't meet, however far they go,
and they are always the same distance apart.

A1 How can you tell by counting grid squares that line *a* is not parallel to line *b*?

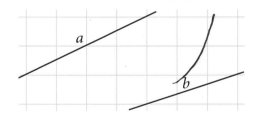

A2 (a) Are lines *p* and *q* parallel to one another?
Explain your answer.

(b) Are lines *r* and *s* parallel to one another?
Explain your answer.

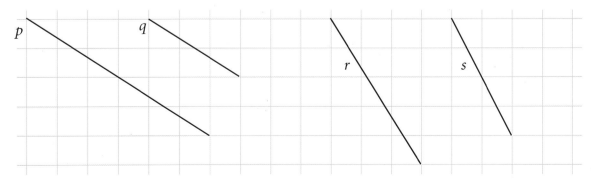

A3 Sort these into groups of lines that are parallel to one another.

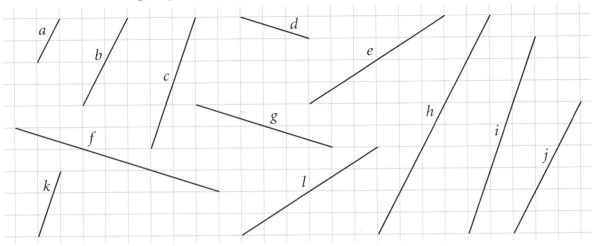

A4 Copy this diagram on to squared paper.

Lines AB and BC are two walls of a garden.
These are the clues to find a buried diamond.

> *Draw a line through P parallel to AB.*
> *Draw a line through Q parallel to BC.*
> *The diamond is where the lines meet.*

Follow the instructions to find
the coordinates of the diamond.

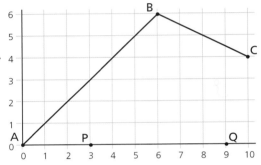

A5 On squared paper, draw axes
from 0 to 17 up and across.

Draw the castle walls as described
in this old document.

Draw where you would walk to
find the treasure.

What are the coordinates of
the place where it is buried?

*Ye walls of ye castle form an irregular hexagon
with its vertices at these points.*

A (1, 12)
B (11, 17)
C (15, 11)
D (10, 1)
E (7, 1)
F (1, 7)

To find ye treasure

Start at point D.
Walk parallel to wall EF until you get to wall AF.
Walk parallel to AB until you get to BC.
Walk parallel to AF until you get to CD.
Walk parallel to DE until you get to EF.
Ye treasure is buried there by the wall.

Try these methods for drawing or checking parallel lines.

1 Measuring along two lines that are perpendicular to your first line

| Draw them using a set square. | Put a mark on each of them the same distance from your first line. | Join the marks. |

2 The sliding set square method

Put an edge of the set square against your first line.

Put a ruler against a different edge of the set square.

Hold the ruler tight and slide the set square along the ruler.

Draw the parallel line.

A6 Do this experiment.

1 Draw a pair of parallel lines (by any method).

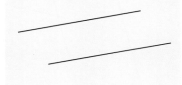

2 Mark points 8 cm apart on one line and 4 cm apart on the other.

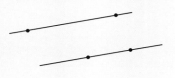

3 Join the points like this. Measure the lengths marked with arrows.

What do you find?

What happens if you mark points 12 cm apart and 4 cm apart?

Try other distances.

B Parallel lines and angles

Think of two pencils in a straight line.

They both rotate 50° clockwise about their ends.

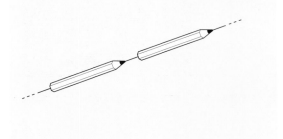

B1 What can you say about these lines?

Think of one pencil.

It rotates 50° anticlockwise about its end …

… then 50° anticlockwise about its point.

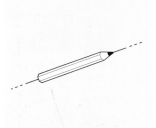

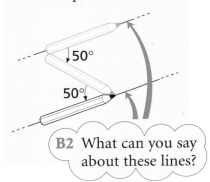

B2 What can you say about these lines?

B3 When a set of parallel lines, all sloping in one direction, crosses another set, sloping in a different direction, you get lots of equal angles.

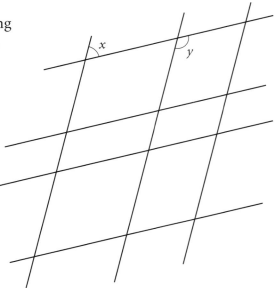

Sketch the diagram.
Mark with an x every angle that equals angle x.
Mark with a y every angle that equals angle y.

B4 You can buy a wooden trellis from a garden centre. It looks like this when you buy it.

You can 'expand' it and hang it on a garden wall so plants can grow up it.

(a) If this angle is 50°, what will the angles marked with letters be?

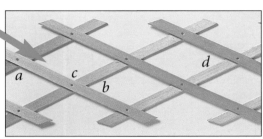

(b) If this angle is 110°, what will the angles marked with letters be?

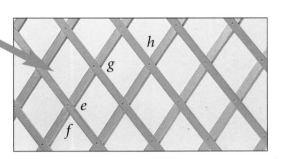

(c) If this angle is 72°, what will the angles marked with letters be?

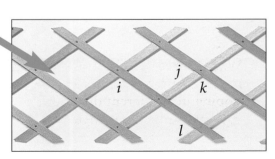

B5 In this diagram, lines of the same colour are parallel to each other. What are the angles marked with letters?

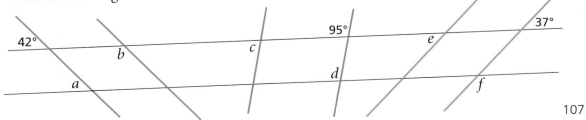

C Related angles

Where two lines cross, there are two pairs of **vertically opposite** angles.
Vertically opposite angles are equal.

Angles which add up to 180° are called **supplementary** angles.
Each pair *x*, *y* in the diagram above is a pair of supplementary angles.

$$x + y = 180°$$

A line that crosses a pair of parallel lines
is sometimes called a **transversal**.

The angles labelled *a* are equal.
They are called **corresponding** angles.

We use arrows to show that lines are parallel.

There are other pairs of corresponding angles in the diagram.

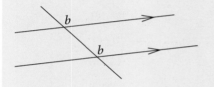 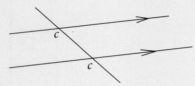 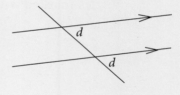

The angles labelled *e* are equal.
They are called **alternate** angles.

There is another pair of alternate angles in the diagram.

The two angles inside the parallel lines on the same side
of the transversal are supplementary.

This is because there is an angle corresponding to *e* which
makes a supplementary pair with *f*.

$$e + f = 180°$$

$$e + f = 180°$$

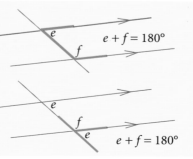

Vertically opposite   Coesponding

Alterate   Spplemenary

C1 Which word completes each sentence?

(a)    Angles *a* and *b* are .... angles.

(b) 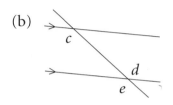   Angles *c* and *d* are .... angles.
Angles *c* and *e* are .... angles.
Angles *d* and *e* are .... angles.

(c) 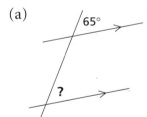   Angles *f* and *g* are .... angles.
Angles *f* and *h* are .... angles.
Angles *g* and *h* are .... angles.
Angles *g* and *i* are .... angles.

C2 Work out each angle marked with a '**?**'.
Give the reason (corresponding, alternate, vertically opposite, supplementary).

(a)

(b)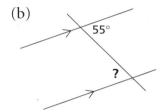

(c)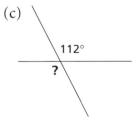

(d)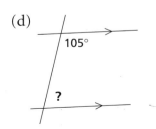

(e)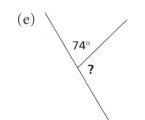

(f)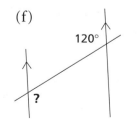

D Explaining how you work out angles

Example

Work out angle x, giving reasons.

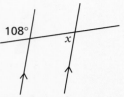

Angle x is not directly related to the angle of 108°.
We need to label another angle in order to explain the steps of the working.

So the diagram is copied to show this other angle, labelled y.

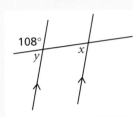

$y + 108° = 180°$ (angles on a straight line)

So $y = 72°$

$x = y$ (corresponding angles)

So $x = \mathbf{72°}$

In questions D1 to D3, copy each sketch.
Work out the angles marked with letters, explaining the reason for each step.
You may need to label other angles as well. Choose your own letters.

D1 (a)   (b)   (c)

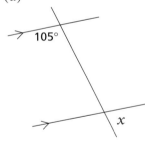

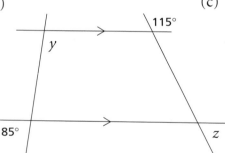

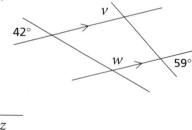

If there is a second set of parallel lines in a diagram, we use double arrows.

D2 (a)   (b)   (c)

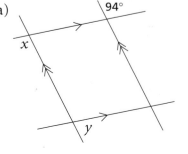

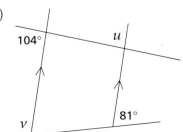

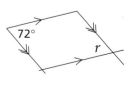

D3 (a)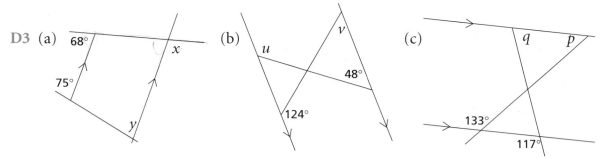

D4 Work out the angles marked with a letter, explaining each result.
If you need to, copy the sketch and add extra lines and angles.

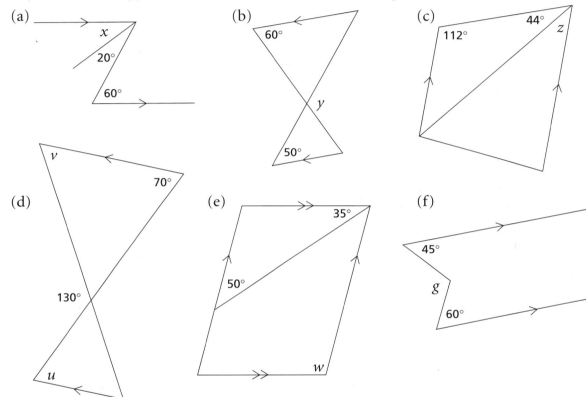

D5 Copy this sketch.
Find two angles that will be equal and label each of them *x*.
Find two more that will be equal and label them *y*.

What does this tell you about the angles of a triangle?

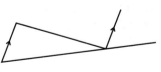

D6 Copy this sketch.

Explain how you can use it to prove
that the angles of a triangle add up to 180°.

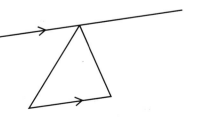

111

D7 Work out the angles marked with letters, giving reasons.

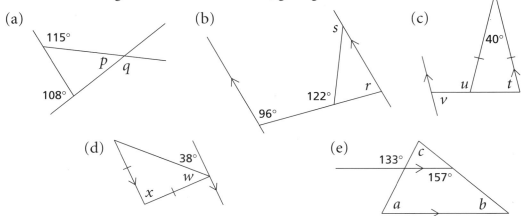

(a) 115° 108° p q

(b) s 96° 122° r

(c) 40° u t v

(d) 38° w x

(e) 133° c 157° a b

Using labelled points

If points in a diagram are labelled with letters, you can use these in your explanations.

Example

Work out angle CBE.

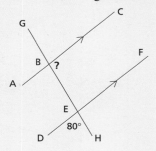

Angle ABE = angle DEH = 80° (corresponding angles)

Angle ABE + angle CBE = 180° (angles on a straight line)

So angle CBE = **100°**

D8 Work out the angles marked with question marks (**?**).
Explain each result.

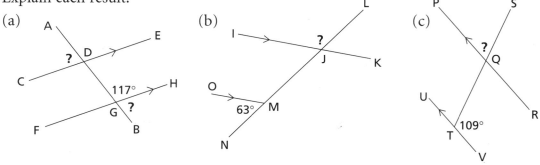

(a) A C D E ? F G 117° ? B H

(b) I L ? J K O 63° M N

(c) P S U ? Q T 109° R V

D9 If the angles shown in this sketch are drawn accurately, which lines will be parallel? Explain how you decided.

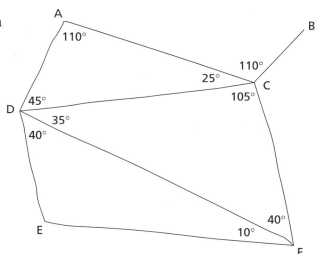

What progress have you made?

Statement	Evidence

I can draw parallel lines.

1 Draw two parallel lines 4 cm apart.

I can tell whether lines on a grid are parallel.

2 Decide whether these two lines are parallel. Explain your answer.

I can work out angles when I know that some lines are parallel.

3 Work out the angles marked with letters.

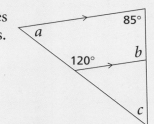

I can give reasons when calculating angles.

4 Work out the angles marked with '?'. Give reasons.

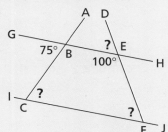

⑮ Percentage

This work will help you
- ◆ change a percentage to a decimal
- ◆ calculate a percentage of a quantity
- ◆ calculate one quantity as a percentage of another
- ◆ construct pie charts

A Understanding percentages

For group work

Most cheeses contain fat, some more than others.
Put these cheeses in order of the proportion of fat in them.

Start with the cheese having the highest proportion of fat.

Danish Blue is 28% fat.

50 g of Blue Stilton contains 18 g of fat.

A 20 g piece of Edam has 5 g of fat in it.

21% of Camembert is fat.

There is 18 g of fat in 40 g of Mascarpone.

Red Leicester is one third fat.

2% of Cottage Cheese is fat.

1 kg of Quark contains 2 g of fat.

114

A1 This bar shows the nutritional content of processed cheese.

0% 10% 20% 30% 40% 50% 60% 70% 80% 90% **100%**

| fat | protein | water | other |

(a) What percentage of processed cheese is fat?

(b) What makes up the greatest part of processed cheese?

(c) What percentage of processed cheese is protein?

A2 (a) Which of these bars are 20% shaded? (There may be more than one.)

(b) Which bars are 40% shaded?

(c) Which bars are 60% shaded?

(d) Which bars are 80% shaded?

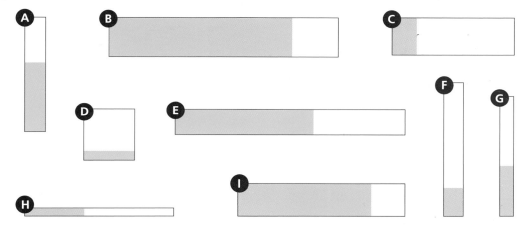

A3 Estimate what percentage each of these bars is shaded.

(a)

(b)

(c)   (d)

(e)

B Percentages in your head

B1 50% of something is the same as $\frac{1}{2}$ of it.

What fraction is the same as

(a) 25%   (b) 75%   (c) 10%   (d) 90%   (e) 20%

B2 Write the proportions in these statements as percentages.
(Some of them may have to be approximations.)

(a) About half of cream cheese is fat.

(b) About $\frac{1}{10}$ of a slice of granary bread is protein.

(c) 1 part in 4 of brown toast is water.

(d) Three quarters of custard is water.

(e) Although about one third of Double Gloucester cheese is fat,
a quarter is protein.

B3 Work these out in your head.

(a) 50% of £30   (b) 50% of £84   (c) 50% of £35

B4 Work these out in your head.

(a) 25% of £40   (b) 25% of £84   (c) 25% of £70

B5 (a) Explain how you work out 10% of a number in your head.
Use 10% of 60 and 10% of 65 as examples.

(b) How do you work out 5% of a number in your head?
Find out from some other people how they do it.

B6 (a) What is 1% of £1?

(b) So what is 3% of £1?

(c) What is 37% of £1?

B7 In 2000 the rate of VAT on goods was 17.5%.
Here is how Anita works out 17.5% of £80 in her head.
Use the method to work out 17.5% of

(a) £60   (b) £220

10% of £80 is   £8
So 5% (half of 10%) is   £4
So 2.5% (half of 5%) is £2
So 17.5% of £80 is   £14

C Percentages and decimals

This diagram shows a bar representing 1 unit.
It is divided up to show fractions, decimals and percentages.

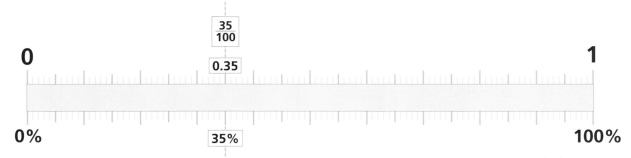

35% of something means the same as $\frac{35}{100}$ of it.

But $\frac{35}{100}$ as a decimal is 0.35, so **35% is equal to 0.35**.

C1 What decimal is equal to
   (a) 50%   (b) 25%   (c) 65%   (d) 78%
   (e) 10%   (f) 1%   (g) 4%   (h) 40%

C2 Copy and complete this table.

Fraction		Decimal		Percentage
$\frac{45}{100}$	=		=	
	=	0.57	=	
$\frac{5}{100}$	=		=	
	=		=	63%
	=	0.07	=	

C3 What percentage is equal to
   (a) 0.3   (b) 0.8   (c) 0.83   (d) 0.03

C4 Put these in order, starting with the smallest.
   0.1   15%   0.25 $\frac{12}{100}$ 1% $\frac{45}{100}$ 0.3

117

D Calculating a percentage of a quantity

There are different types of fat, but for a balanced diet
it helps to know how much fat we are eating.

This Stilton cheese is 35% fat.
I wonder how much fat there is in a 40 g piece?

Joe works out 35% of 40 g like this:

35% of 40 g

= $\frac{35}{100} \times 40$ g ← You can leave out this step.

= 0.35 × 40 g

= 14 g

D1 Calculate these.
(a) 45% of 360 g   (b) 61% of 420 g   (c) 29% of 230 g   (d) 70% of 134 g
(e) 14% of 190 g   (f) 22% of 160 g   (g) 96% of 210 g   (h) 11% of 480 g

D2 Calculate these.
(a) 3% of 75 g   (b) 7% of 96 g   (c) 8% of 45 g   (d) 6% of 28 g

D3 White bread is 2% fat. How much fat is there in a 30 g slice?

D4 Fred said: 'Percentages? Easy! To find 10%, just divide by 10.
For 5%, just divide by 5, and so on.'
Quickly convince Fred that he is wrong.

D5 This **pie chart** shows the nutritional content of
milk chocolate.

Calculate the amounts of sugar, fat and protein in
(a) a 35 g bar
(b) a 150 g bar
(c) a 500 g bar

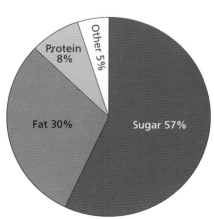

E Changing fractions to decimals

The fraction $\frac{1}{5}$ means 1 unit divided by 5.

Doing $1 \div 5$ on a calculator gives 0.2,
which is the **decimal equivalent** of $\frac{1}{5}$.

The fraction $\frac{2}{5}$ can be thought of as 2 times $\frac{1}{5}$.

It can also be thought of as **2 units divided by 5**.
You can look at it this way.

2 pizzas are to be shared equally between 5 people.
Each pizza is cut into fifths.

Each person gets $\frac{1}{5}$ of the first
pizza and $\frac{1}{5}$ of the second.

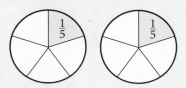

That's $\frac{2}{5}$ altogether for each
person.

So $2 \div 5 = \frac{2}{5}$

So to change $\frac{2}{5}$ to a decimal, **divide 2 by 5**: $\quad \frac{2}{5} = 2 \div 5 = \textbf{0.4}$

E1 Change each of these fractions to decimals.

(a) $\frac{1}{4}$ (b) $\frac{1}{8}$ (c) $\frac{1}{20}$ (d) $\frac{4}{5}$ (e) $\frac{3}{8}$

(f) $\frac{7}{8}$ (g) $\frac{7}{25}$ (h) $\frac{3}{20}$ (i) $\frac{11}{50}$ (j) $\frac{15}{16}$

E2 Put these fractions in order of size, smallest first.

$$\frac{5}{8} \quad \frac{3}{5} \quad \frac{13}{20} \quad \frac{29}{50}$$

E3 Change each of these fractions to a decimal.
Round them to two decimal places.

(a) $\frac{1}{7}$ (b) $\frac{4}{7}$ (c) $\frac{1}{9}$ (d) $\frac{5}{9}$ (e) $\frac{7}{11}$

(f) $\frac{4}{15}$ (g) $\frac{1}{13}$ (h) $\frac{5}{13}$ (i) $\frac{7}{17}$ (j) $\frac{20}{23}$

F One number as a percentage of another

Problem 3 out of 7 jelly babies are red.
What percentage of the jelly babies are red?

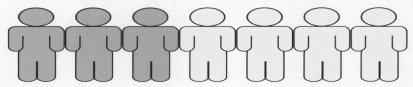

Solution $\frac{3}{7}$ of the jelly babies are red.

(Change the fraction to a decimal ...) (and the decimal to a percentage.)

$\frac{3}{7}$ = 3 ÷ 7 = [ ] = 42.85714 ...% = **43%**

to the nearest 1%

This diagram shows that the answer is right.

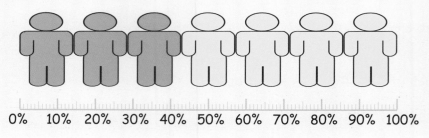

0% 10% 20% 30% 40% 50% 60% 70% 80% 90% 100%

F1 Five out of seven jelly babies are red.

What percentage of the jelly babies are red?
Check your answer using the diagram above.

F2 Match together these fractions and percentages. Some percentages are left over!

(a) $\frac{3}{5}$ (b) $\frac{7}{20}$ (c) $\frac{7}{8}$ (d) $\frac{1}{3}$ (e) $\frac{2}{3}$

| 3% | 3.5% | 6% | 35% | |
| | | | | 60% |

about 33%   about 67%   87.5%

F3 Change these fractions into percentages, to the nearest 1%.

(a) $\frac{2}{7}$ (b) $\frac{7}{9}$ (c) $\frac{3}{13}$ (d) $\frac{7}{17}$ (e) $\frac{1}{19}$

In questions F4 to F7, round percentages to the nearest 1%.

F4 In a survey Kim asked her friends what their favourite vegetable was.
    She asked a total of 32 people; 8 said potatoes and 6 said carrots.
    (a) What fraction of Kim's friends said potatoes?
    (b) What percentage said potatoes?   (c) What percentage said carrots?

F5 Frank buys 23 tomatoes of which 7 are bad.
    What percentage of the tomatoes are bad?

F6 Tina suggests this method
    of checking percentages.
    Does this method work?

    I calculated 21 out of 60 as a percentage and got 35%.
    If I'm right, then 35% of 60 should be 21.

    Make up and test some calculations of your own.

F7 The world's population is about 6000 million.
    It is reckoned that 950 million people are hungry all the time.
    (a) What percentage of the world are hungry all the time?
    (b) Imagine that the people in your class represent all the people in the world.
         How many of them would be hungry all the time?

Worked example   On a farm of 12.4 km², 5.1 km² are used for growing wheat.
                      What percentage of the farm is used for growing wheat?

If the numbers were 12 and 5, you would do 5 ÷ 12 = 0.416... = 42%, to the nearest 1%.
Do the same for the actual numbers.

5.1 ÷ 12.4 = 0.411... = **41%**, to the nearest 1%.

F8 Check that 41% of 12.4 is about 5.1 .

F9 Calculate each of these as a percentage, to the nearest 1%.
    (a) 4.2 out of 6.6   (b) 3.8 out of 7.1   (c) 10.4 out of 13.7
    (d) 0.6 out of 1.7   (e) 4.24 out of 5.72   (f) 0.73 out of 1.06

F10 Two samples of low fat cheese were tested for their fat content.
    13.7 g of cheese A contained 1.92 g of fat.
    17.1 g of cheese B contained 2.65 g of fat.
    Which cheese sample had the higher percentage of fat?

G Drawing pie charts

You need a pie chart scale.

Pie charts are often a good way of displaying percentage information.
They are very useful when making comparisons.
For example, these pie charts show the nutritional content of cheese slices and cheese spread.

Nutritional content of cheese slices

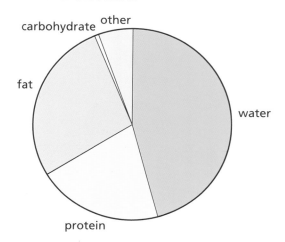

Nutritional content of cheese spread

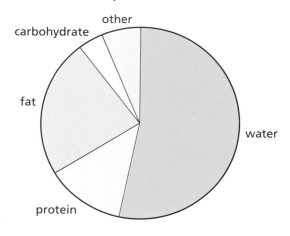

G1 Write in a couple of sentences what you can see from the pie charts.

G2 The actual percentages may be read off from a pie chart using a pie chart scale.

Use a pie chart scale to find these percentages from the two pie charts above.

(a) fat in cheese slices

(b) fat in cheese spread

(c) water in cheese slices

(d) water in cheese spread

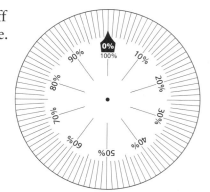

G3 Use a pie chart scale to draw a pie chart to illustrate this data.

Nutritional content of cheese and tomato pizza				
Water	Protein	Fat	Carbohydrate	Other
52%	9%	12%	25%	2%

G4 This pie chart shows how the average household in England in 1995 spent money on types of food.

(a) Which type of food was most money spent on?

(b) What percentage was spent on fruit?

(c) Clio looked at the pie chart and said, 'People ate about twice as much meat, fish and eggs as they did vegetables.' Is this a reasonable conclusion?

G5 Here is how the Siddiqi family spent money on food in one week.

(a) Calculate the percentage of the total food bill which is spent on each type of food.

(b) Draw a pie chart to illustrate the data.

Milk, butter, dairy products	£ 8
Meat, fish, eggs	£28
Vegetables	£12
Fruit	£ 8
Bread, cakes, cereals	£20
Sugar, sweets, jams, fats, oils	£ 4
Total	**£80**

G6 This table shows how the pages of a newspaper were allocated.

	Home news	Foreign news	Sport	Entertainment	Finance
Number of pages	11	7	5	3	6

(a) What percentage of the total number of pages were devoted to home news? Give your answer to the nearest 1%.

(b) Calculate the percentage for each of the other headings and draw a pie chart.

G7 This table gives information about Parinda's CD collection.

	Pop	Hard rock	Jazz	Easy listening	Classical
Number of CDs	13	4	8	3	9

Draw a pie chart to show this information.
Label each slice with its percentage.

H Problems involving percentages

H1 A carton of orange juice normally contains 250 ml.
In a special offer, 15% extra is given 'free'.

How much juice is there in the special offer carton?

H2 A piece of cheese contains 12 g of fat.
According to the label the cheese is 30% fat.

What is the weight of the piece of cheese?

H3 This table shows the fat and protein content of three types of cheese.

	Protein	Fat
Cheese A	15%	30%
Cheese B	40%	30%
Cheese C	50%	25%

Peter is on a diet in which he needs at least 30 g of protein but not more than 20 g of fat.

(a) Could he get these amounts by eating some of cheese A?

(b) Could either of cheese B or C give him enough protein but not too much fat?

H4 Purity of gold is measured in carats. 24 carat is 100% pure.
So 6 carat is $\frac{6}{24}$ pure, and so on.

What percentage (to the nearest 0.1%) of pure gold is there in

(a) 12 carat ring   (b) a 9 carat brooch

(c) a 22 carat coin   (d) a 14 carat nib

H5 In a school, 20% of the boys and 5% of the girls play football regularly.
There are 450 boys and 500 girls in the school.

What percentage of all the pupils play football regularly?

H6 Look at the completed 'of' square.
Make sure you understand how it works.

of	100	50	200
10%	10	5	20
20%	20	10	40
50%	50	25	100

Then copy and complete the other two squares.

(a)

of	20		50	
5%		0.5		
	0.2	0.1	0.5	
8%		0.8		

(b)

of	50		80	
15%			12	
	45	27		
	0.5		0.8	

What progress have you made?

Statement	Evidence

Statement

Evidence

I understand what percentage means.

1 Which of these bars is

(a) about 40% shaded

(b) about 20% shaded

(c) about 60% shaded

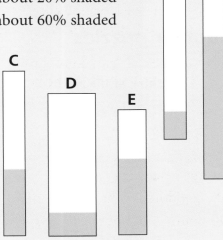

I can change percentages into decimals.

2 Change these percentages into decimals.

(a) 50% (b) 45% (c) 4% (d) 7%

I can calculate percentages of quantities, both in my head and using a calculator.

3 Calculate these in your head.

(a) 50% of £10 (b) 25% of 8 kg

(c) 75% of 12 kg (d) 10% of £20

4 Calculate these.

(a) 38% of 180 g (b) 4% of 325 g

I can calculate one quantity as a percentage of another.

5 Ann has 44 apple trees. 32 of them are affected by a disease.
What percentage of the trees are affected?

6 Which is the better record,
21 successes out of 25 tries, or 30 out of 37?
Explain why.

I can draw a pie chart.

7 Draw a percentage pie chart to show this information about a football team.

Wins: 24   Losses: 6   Draws: 10

16 Think of a number

This work will help you

◆ solve 'think of a number' puzzles by using inverses
◆ solve equations using inverses

A Number puzzles

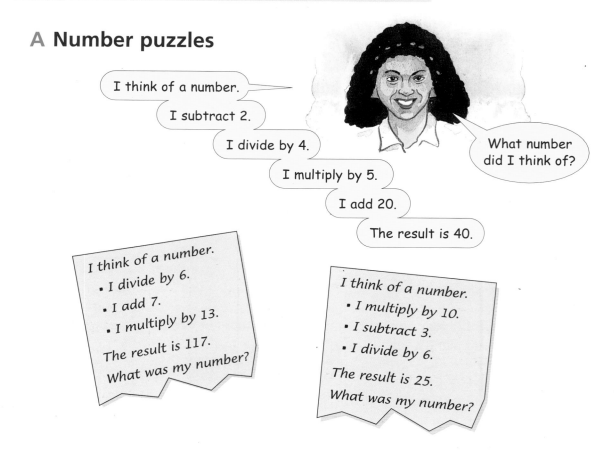

I think of a number.

I subtract 2.

I divide by 4.

I multiply by 5.

I add 20.

The result is 40.

What number did I think of?

I think of a number.
• I divide by 6.
• I add 7.
• I multiply by 13.
The result is 117.
What was my number?

I think of a number.
• I multiply by 10.
• I subtract 3.
• I divide by 6.
The result is 25.
What was my number?

A1 To solve a puzzle, Pat has drawn an arrow diagram and reversed it.

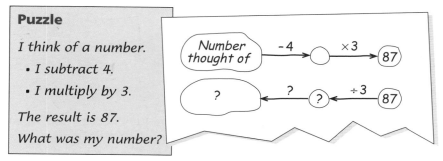

Puzzle

I think of a number.
• I subtract 4.
• I multiply by 3.
The result is 87.
What was my number?

Number thought of → −4 → ○ → ×3 → 87

? ← ? ← ? ← ÷3 ← 87

Copy and complete Pat's diagram and solve the puzzle.

A2 (a) Match each of these puzzles to an arrow diagram.

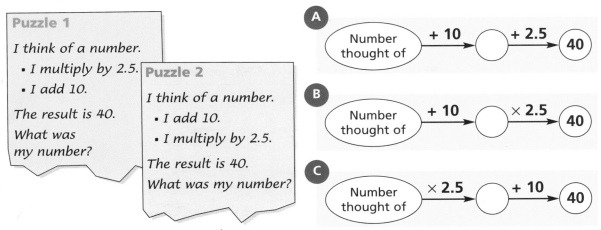

Puzzle 1

I think of a number.
• I multiply by 2.5.
• I add 10.

The result is 40.
What was my number?

Puzzle 2

I think of a number.
• I add 10.
• I multiply by 2.5.

The result is 40.
What was my number?

A Number thought of →+ 10→ ○ →+ 2.5→ 40

B Number thought of →+ 10→ ○ →× 2.5→ 40

C Number thought of →× 2.5→ ○ →+ 10→ 40

(b) Solve these puzzles by reversing their arrow diagrams.

A3 (a) Write a puzzle to match this arrow diagram.
(b) Solve the puzzle by reversing the arrow diagram.

Number thought of →÷ 4→ ○ →− 1→ 1.5

A4 Solve these puzzles using arrow diagrams.

(a) I think of a number.
• I subtract 5.
• I multiply by 8.2.

The result is 123.
What was my number?

(b) I think of a number.
• I divide by 12.
• I add 2.5.
• I multiply by 0.5.

The result is 5.
What was my number?

(c) I think of a number.
• I add 3.
• I divide by 0.2.
• I subtract 20.

The result is 7.
What was my number?

A5 I think of a number.
• I add 🌸
• I multiply by 🌸

The result is 12.
What was my number?

Jason makes up this number puzzle.

The number Jason thought of was 2.
What could the hidden numbers be in his puzzle?

A6 The result for this number puzzle is missing.

(a) Choose a number for the result.
Solve the number puzzle for your result.
(b) Solve the number puzzle for some different results.
(c) What do you notice? Try to explain this.

I think of a number.
• I subtract 1.
• I multiply by 6.
• I add 3.
• I divide by 3.
• I add 1.
• I divide by 2.

The result is

What was my number?

B Using letters

Here is a number puzzle.

> I think of a number.
> I add 3 and then multiply by 2.
>
> The result is 20. What was my number?

We can use a letter to stand for
the number thought of.
The letter *n* is used here.

In the diagram we can show
what happens to *n*.

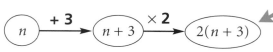

> Brackets show
> that you work out
> *n* + 3 first.

So this number puzzle can be written $2(n + 3) = 20$

> This is called
> an **equation**.

B1 (a) Match each arrow diagram with an equation.

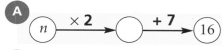

A

$n \xrightarrow{\times 2} \bigcirc \xrightarrow{+ 7} 16$

B

$n \xrightarrow{+ 7} \bigcirc \xrightarrow{\times 2} 16$

C

$n \xrightarrow{\times 7} \bigcirc \xrightarrow{+ 2} 16$

D

$n \xrightarrow{+ 7} \bigcirc \xrightarrow{\times 5} 16$

V $7n + 2 = 16$

W $2(n + 7) = 16$

X $5(n + 7) = 16$

Y $2n + 7 = 16$

Z $5n + 7 = 16$

(b) Draw an arrow diagram for the unmatched equation.

B2 (a) Match each number puzzle with an equation.

W
> I think of a number.
> • I multiply by 4.
> • I subtract 5.
> The result is 8.
> What was my number?

X
> I think of a number.
> • I subtract 5.
> • I divide by 4.
> The result is 8.
> What was my number?

Y
> I think of a number.
> • I add 1.
> • I divide by 4.
> The result is 8.
> What was my number?

Z
> I think of a number.
> • I divide by 4.
> • I add 1.
> The result is 8.
> What was my number?

A $4(x - 5) = 8$

B $\dfrac{m - 5}{4} = 8$

C $\dfrac{p}{4} + 1 = 8$

D $4y - 5 = 8$

E $\dfrac{q + 1}{4} = 8$

(b) Write a puzzle for the unmatched equation.

B3 Write an equation for each of these number puzzles.

Use n to stand for the number each time.

(a) | *I think of a number.*
• I multiply by 3.
• I add 4.
The result is 108.
What was my number?

(b) | *I think of a number.*
• I multiply by 4.5.
The result is 162.
What was my number?

(c) | *I think of a number.*
• I subtract 2.
• I divide by 5.
The result is 2.2.
What was my number?

B4 Write an equation for each arrow diagram.

(a) n $\xrightarrow{\div 3}$ ○ $\xrightarrow{+6}$ 21
(b) k $\xrightarrow{-5}$ ○ $\xrightarrow{\times 2.6}$ 65

C Solving equations

Solving an equation by using arrow diagrams

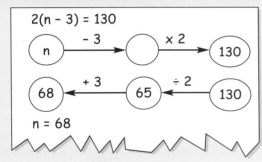

$2(n - 3) = 130$

n $\xrightarrow{-3}$ ○ $\xrightarrow{\times 2}$ 130

68 $\xleftarrow{+3}$ 65 $\xleftarrow{\div 2}$ 130

$n = 68$

Check
When n = 68,
2(n – 3) = 2 × (68 – 3)
= 2 × 65 = 130 ✓

C1 Solve these equations by using arrow diagrams. Check your solutions.

(a) $5n - 3 = 57$ (b) $13(h + 9) = 247$ (c) $15p + 3 = 318$

(d) $\dfrac{q + 4}{3} = 25$ (e) $\dfrac{t}{7} - 1 = 1.4$ (f) $\dfrac{s - 2}{5} = 3.4$

C2 Solve these equations. Check your solutions.

(a) $6n - 2.4 = 42$ (b) $5p + 0.5 = 20$ (c) $0.5q - 6 = 10$

(d) $\dfrac{x}{9} + 3.6 = 4$ (e) $\dfrac{y - 12.1}{2} = 5$ (f) $\dfrac{z}{8} - 0.2 = 1$

C3 Check that $n = 6$ is a solution to $\dfrac{n - 3}{5} = 0.6$.

Make up three different equations with $n = 6$ as a solution.

C4 Make up two different equations that have $y = 1.5$ as a solution.

C5 Solve these equations.

(a) $2(m - 5) + 9 = 45$ (b) $4.5(p + 2.3) - 5.6 = 7.9$

(c) $\dfrac{s + 4}{1.5} - 6 = 3$ (d) $\dfrac{7t}{0.35} + 1 = 2$

129

D Quick solve game   for a group of three or four players

- Each group needs the three sets of cards from sheet 157.
- Shuffle each set and put each in a pile face down.
  You now have a 1-point pile, a 2-point pile and a 3-point pile.
- Each player chooses a pile, takes the top card and tries to solve the equation.
- Whenever a player thinks they have solved an equation,
  they take another card from any pile.
- When all the cards are used up, check each other's solutions.
  A correct solution wins the number of points on the card.
  A point is lost for any incorrect solution.

What progress have you made?

Statement	Evidence

I can solve 'think of a number' puzzles using arrow diagrams.

1 Solve these puzzles by using arrow diagrams.

(a)
> I think of a number.
> - I multiply by 25.
> - I take away 7.5.
>
> The result is 35.
> What was my number?

(b)
> I think of a number.
> - I add 10.
> - I divide by 2.3.
> - I subtract 5.
>
> The result is 38.
> What was my number?

I can match arrow diagrams and equations.

2 Match each arrow diagram with an equation.

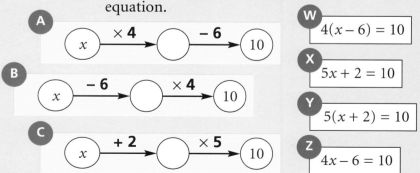

A x → ×4 → ○ → −6 → 10

B x → −6 → ○ → ×4 → 10

C x → +2 → ○ → ×5 → 10

W $4(x - 6) = 10$

X $5x + 2 = 10$

Y $5(x + 2) = 10$

Z $4x - 6 = 10$

I can solve equations.

3 Solve these equations.

(a) $3.7z - 5 = 69$ (b) $5(p + 3) = 105$

(c) $\frac{y}{4} - 7 = 17$ (d) $\frac{q + 0.3}{0.5} = 8$

(e) $\frac{2x}{5.9} + 7.2 = 9$

Quadrilaterals

This work will help you

◆ recognise special quadrilaterals (shapes with four straight sides)
◆ draw them
◆ learn about their properties
◆ see that some quadrilaterals are special types of other quadrilaterals

A Special quadrilaterals

These are special quadrilaterals.
What is special about each one?

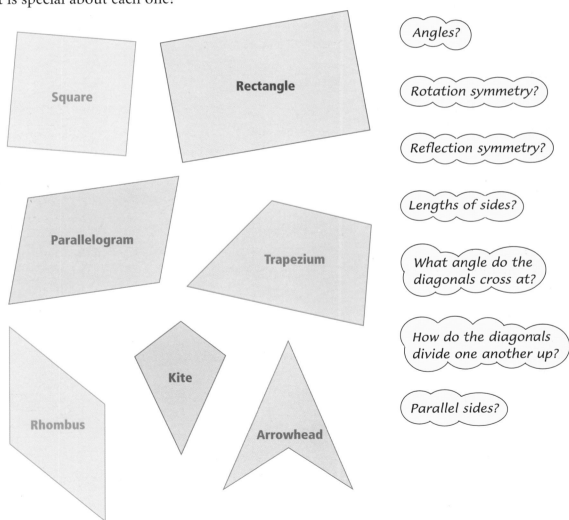

Square

Rectangle

Parallelogram

Trapezium

Kite

Rhombus

Arrowhead

Angles?

Rotation symmetry?

Reflection symmetry?

Lengths of sides?

What angle do the diagonals cross at?

How do the diagonals divide one another up?

Parallel sides?

131

A1 These are two sides of a rectangle.
Draw them on dotty paper.

Now finish the rectangle.

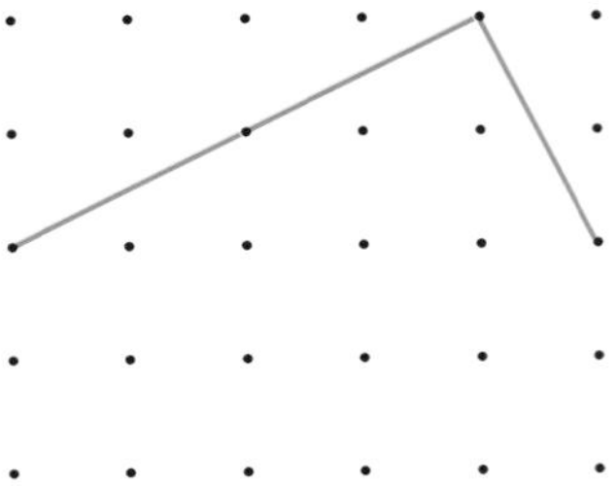

A2 Now do the same with these quadrilaterals.

(a)

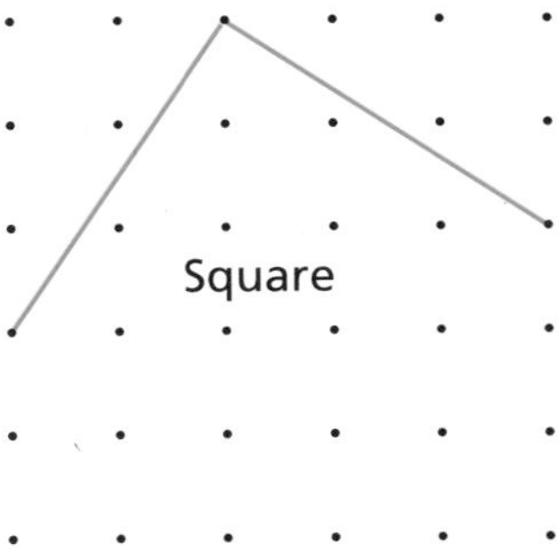

Square

(b)

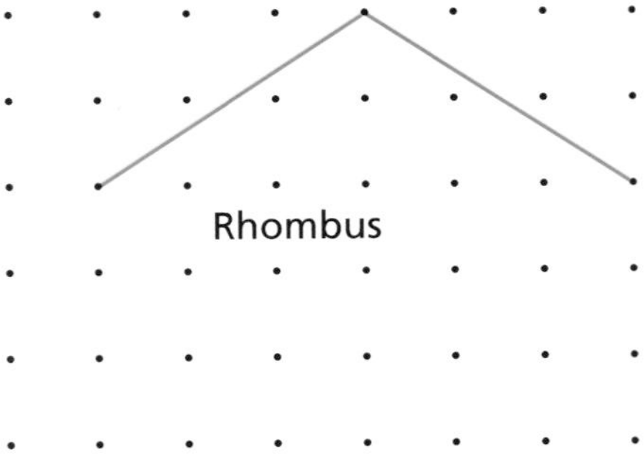

Rhombus

(c)

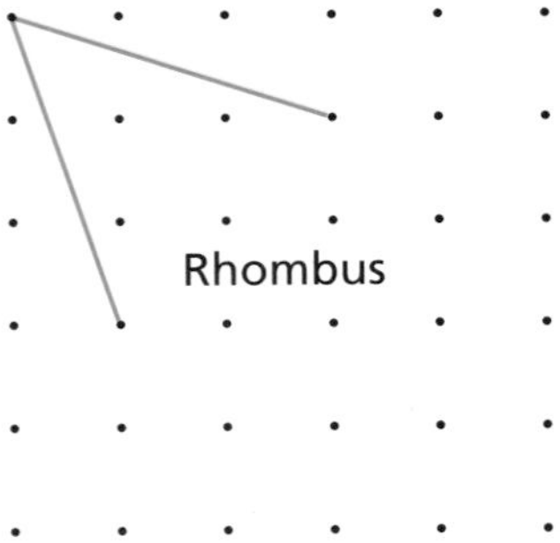

Rhombus

(d)

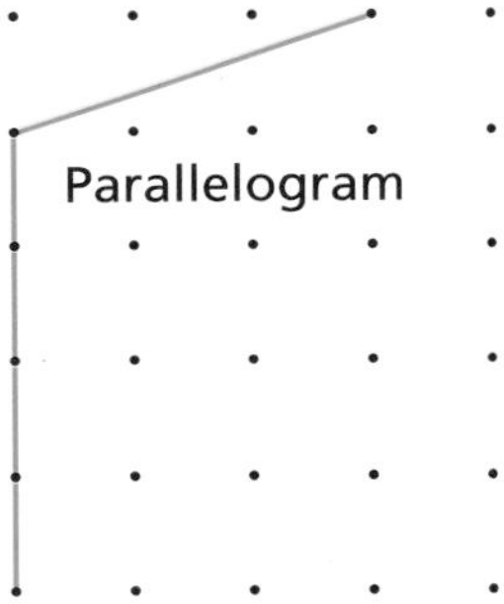

Parallelogram

(e)

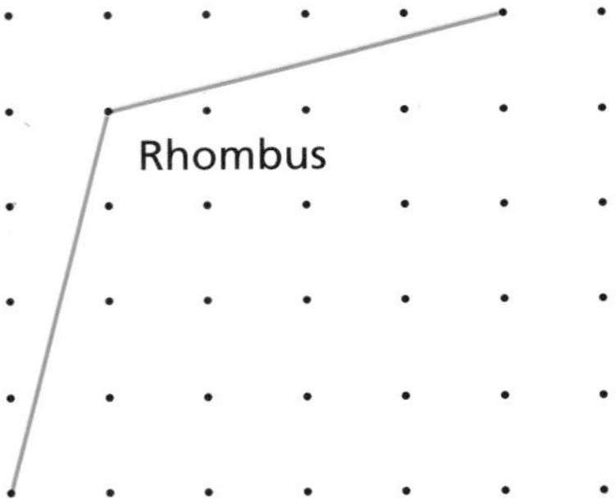

Rhombus

(f)

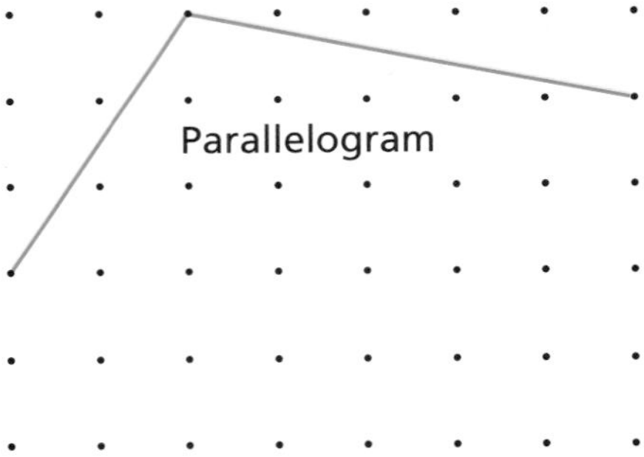

Parallelogram

A3 Complete these two sides to make
(a) a kite
(b) a parallelogram

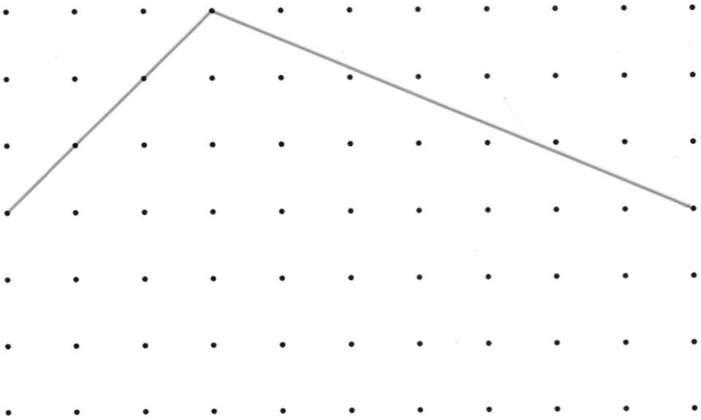

A4 On dotty paper, draw two dots positioned like these.

Draw a square with your dots as two of its vertices.

Can you draw a square of a different size with these dots as vertices?

A5 Draw a rhombus with a line like this as a **diagonal**.

Can you draw only one?

A6 This line is a diagonal of a rhombus. The area of the rhombus is 12 square units.

Draw the rhombus.
Can you only draw one?

A7 This is a diagonal of a kite. Its area is 16 square units.

Draw it.
Can you only draw one?

A8 These are two sides of a trapezium. Its area is 20 square units.

Draw it.
Can you only draw one?

B Quadrilaterals from triangles

Use the triangles on sheet 164.

B1 Cut out the two scalene triangles
with no right angle.

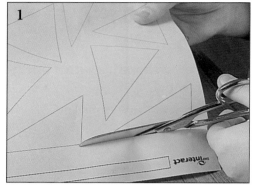

Fit them together on your exercise
book to make a quadrilateral.

Draw round it carefully.

Draw in a diagonal to show how it was
made from the triangles.

Label your quadrilateral to show
what kind it is.

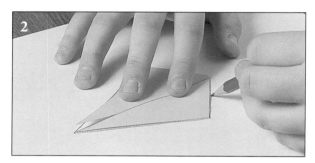

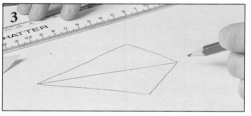

Make as many different quadrilaterals as you can with these two scalene triangles.
Draw round each quadrilateral, and draw a diagonal to show how it was made.
Label each quadrilateral with its name.

B2 If your scalene triangles had been shaped like this,
which of the quadrilaterals could you not make?

B3 Cut out the two isosceles triangles.
Use the same method to draw as many quadrilaterals as you can.
Show how each one was made and write its name.

B4 If your isosceles triangle had been like this,
what difference would it have made?

⑱ Negative numbers

This work will help you

◆ multiply and divide negative numbers

◆ understand positive and negative square roots

A Addition and subtraction patterns

A
5 + 4 = 9
5 + 3 = 8
5 + 2 = 7
5 + 1 =
5 + 0 =
5 + ⁻1 =
5 + ⁻2 =
...

B
⁻3 + 4 = 1
⁻3 + 3 = 0
⁻3 + 2 = ⁻1
⁻3 + 1 =
⁻3 + 0 =
⁻3 + ⁻1 =
⁻3 + ⁻2 =
...

C
8 − 3 = 5
8 − 2 = 6
8 − 1 = 7
8 − 0 =
8 − ⁻1 =
8 − ⁻2 =
8 − ⁻3 =
...

D
⁻2 − 3 = ⁻5
⁻2 − 2 = ⁻4
⁻2 − 1 = ⁻3
⁻2 − 0 =
⁻2 − ⁻1 =
⁻2 − ⁻2 =
⁻2 − ⁻3 =
...

A1 Work these out.

   (a) 7 + ⁻2   (b) 7 − ⁻2   (c) 10 − ⁻6   (d) 3 + ⁻7   (e) 12 − ⁻4

A2 Work these out.

   (a) ⁻3 + 7   (b) ⁻3 − 2   (c) ⁻4 + 9   (d) ⁻3 + ⁻2   (e) 7 + ⁻4

A3 Work these out.

   (a) ⁻6 − ⁻2   (b) ⁻3 − ⁻4   (c) ⁻7 + ⁻9   (d) 11 − ⁻2   (e) ⁻7 − ⁻10

A4 You have these cards.

⁻2 ⁻4 ⁻5 1 3 7

How many different additions and subtractions can you make using cards from this set? (A card can be used once only in each calculation.)

Here are two examples.

        ⁻5 + 1 = ⁻4   3 − ⁻4 = 7

B Multiplication

How can we extend this table?

×	⁻4	⁻3	⁻2	⁻1	0	1	2	3	4
4					0	4	8	12	16
3					0	3	6	9	12
2					0	2	4	6	8
1					0	1	2	3	4
0					0	0	0	0	0
⁻1									
⁻2									
⁻3									
⁻4									

B1 Work these out.

(a) $3 \times {}^-7$ 　 (b) $^-3 \times {}^-7$ 　 (c) $^-5 \times {}^-6$ 　 (d) $8 \times {}^-3$ 　 (e) $^-4 \times {}^-6$

B2 Work these out.

(a) $2 \times {}^-3 \times 5$ 　 (b) $^-4 \times 3 \times {}^-2$ 　 (c) $^-2 \times {}^-5 \times {}^-3$ 　 (d) $8 \times {}^-3 \times 2$

B3 Copy and complete this working to find the value of $12 + 3n$ when $n = {}^-5$.

> $12 + 3n$
> $= 12 + (3 \times {}^-5)$
> $= 12 + \ldots$
> $= \ldots$

B4 Copy and complete this working to find the value of $20 - 4p$ when $p = {}^-3$.

> $20 - 4p$
> $= 20 - (4 \times {}^-3)$
> $= 20 - \ldots$
> $= \ldots$

B5 Find the value of

(a) $^-7 + 4x$ when $x = {}^-2$ 　 (b) $16 - 7y$ when $y = 4$ 　 (c) $13 - 5z$ when $z = {}^-2$

(d) $3(r - 5)$ when $r = {}^-7$ 　 (e) $^-2s + 11$ when $s = {}^-4$ 　 (f) $^-2(t - 9)$ when $t = {}^-8$

B6 Kirsty said, 'I think of a number. I square it. The result is 64. What was my number?' 'Easy,' said Clare. 'Your number must have been 8.'

Was Clare right? If not, why not?

B7 I think of a number, square it and add 5. The result is 21.
What could my number be?

*B8 I think of a number, add 1 and then square. The result is 49.
What could my number be?

C Division

From $3 \times 2 = 6$, we get two divisions: $3 \times 2 = 6$

$$\frac{6}{3} = 2$$

$$\frac{6}{2} = 3$$

C1 Write down the two divisions you get from $4 \times {}^-5 = {}^-20$.

C2 Write down the two divisions you get from ${}^-6 \times {}^-3 = 18$.

C3 Look through your answers to questions C1 and C2.
Copy and complete these rules for dividing positive and negative numbers.

$$\frac{positive}{positive} = positive \qquad \frac{negative}{positive} = \ldots \qquad \frac{positive}{negative} = \ldots \qquad \frac{negative}{negative} = \ldots$$

C4 Work these out.

(a) $\frac{16}{{}^-4}$ (b) $\frac{{}^-20}{{}^-2}$ (c) $\frac{{}^-36}{9}$ (d) $\frac{25}{{}^-5}$ (e) $\frac{{}^-32}{{}^-4}$ (f) $\frac{{}^-40}{{}^-10}$ (g) $\frac{56}{{}^-8}$ (h) $\frac{{}^-45}{9}$

C5 Copy and complete this working to find the value of $10 - \frac{8}{n}$ when $n = {}^-2$.

$$10 - \frac{8}{n}$$
$$= 10 - \frac{8}{{}^-2}$$
$$= 10 - \ldots$$
$$= \ldots$$

C6 Find the value of

(a) ${}^-7 + \frac{4}{x}$ when $x = {}^-2$ (b) $\frac{16}{y} - 7$ when $y = {}^-4$ (c) $13 - \frac{6}{z}$ when $z = {}^-2$

(d) $\frac{24 - 6r}{2}$ when $r = {}^-3$ (e) ${}^-2 - \frac{36}{s}$ when $s = {}^-4$ (f) $\frac{{}^-26 - t}{{}^-9}$ when $t = {}^-8$

C7 (a) What is the output of this arrow diagram?

Input

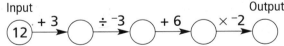

Output

(b) The input stays the same.
Rearrange the order of the four operations so that the output is
(i) 6   (ii) 17   (iii) 5   (iv) 8

C8 Show how to put the numbers ${}^-12$, ${}^-4$, 3 and 24 in the spaces to get the result

(a) 5   (b) 2   (c) ${}^-5$ (d) ${}^-1\frac{1}{4}$

D Using inverse operations

D1 (a) What is the output of this arrow diagram when the input is ⁻5?

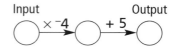

(b) What is the input if the output is

    (i) 33   (ii) ⁻3   (iii) ⁻19

D2 (a) What is the output of this arrow diagram when the input is 13?

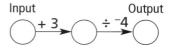

(b) What is the input if the output is

    (i) 7   (ii) ⁻5   (iii) ⁻22

D3 Solve these 'think of a number' problems.

(a) I think of a number. I multiply by ⁻3. I add 4. The result is 25.

(b) I think of a number. I subtract 8. I multiply by ⁻5. The result is 30.

(c) I think of a number. I multiply by ⁻3. I subtract 7. The result is 17.

D4 Solve these 'think of a number' problems.

(a) I think of a number. I divide by ⁻2. I add ⁻7. The result is ⁻5.

(b) I think of a number. I subtract 7. I divide by ⁻3. The result is ⁻6.

(c) I think of a number. I multiply by ⁻0.5. I subtract 8. The result is ⁻1.

What progress have you made?

Statement

I can use all four operations with negative numbers.

Evidence

1 Work these out.

    (a) $5 - {}^-7$ (b) ${}^-4 - 5$ (c) ${}^-8 - {}^-2$

2 Work these out.

    (a) ${}^-4 \times {}^-7$ (b) $3 \times {}^-9$ (c) ${}^-2 \times 8$

    (d) $15 \div {}^-5$ (e) ${}^-32 \div 4$ (f) $35 \div {}^-7$

3 Solve these problems.

    (a) I think of a number. I multiply by ⁻4. I subtract 10. The result is ⁻2. What was my number?

    (b) I think of a number. I subtract 17. I divide by ⁻3. The result is 4. What was my number?

⑲ Fair to all?

This is about using different averages.
The work will help you

◆ calculate the mean of a set of data

◆ choose a suitable average to represent a set of data

A How to be fair

Some pupils in Year 9 held a paper collection competition.

Sharon	10 kg
Amy	6 kg
Rajit	7 kg
Mark	9 kg

Joshua	9 kg
Isha	3 kg
Purva	10 kg
Krush	6 kg
Rik	8 kg
Nina	6 kg

Whose group did better?

A1 Here are the results of rolling a dice.

What is the mean result?

A2 Julie did a survey of how many goldfish her friends had.
Here are her results: 15, 10, 9, 12, 12, 8, 20, 14, 9, 11

What is the mean number of goldfish?

A3 Lewis recorded the number of pupils using the school minibus one week.

Weekdays: Number of pupils each journey 10, 7, 4, 9, 10
Weekend: Number of pupils each journey 11, 8, 11, 6

What was the mean number of pupils
(a) on weekdays   (b) at the weekend

A4 Ruth grows peppers in a growing bag. She has five plants.
She picked a total of 35 peppers.

What was the mean number of peppers per plant?

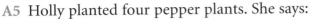

A5 Holly planted four pepper plants. She says:

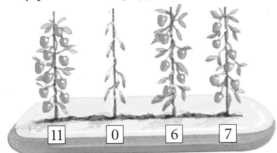

| 11 | 0 | 6 | 7 |

The mean number of peppers on my plants is twenty-four divided by three.

This gives a mean of eight peppers per plant.

But Ruth says the mean is only six peppers.
Who is right and why?

A6 Here are the points scored by three people playing a computer game.
Use these figures to help you decide who you think is the best points scorer.
Give a reason for your choice.

Pat Mitchele	10	7	7	8		
Jon Simpson	11	0	15	8	5	
Wayne Beeza	20	5	10	8	4	4

A7 Forms 8L and 8N collected bottles and cans for recycling.

Here are the record sheets for each form.
They show the number of cans and bottles collected by each person.

```
8L
Cans     2 3 2 5 0 1 2 5 2 0 0 4 3 1 1 2 0 0 6 1
Bottles  1 0 1 3 4 3 3 4 4 2 1 5 4 2 4 1 1 0 4 3
```

```
8N
Cans     1 1 2 1 4 1 1 2 0 3 1 0 4 5 6 1 0 2 3 1 1 3 2 2 8
Bottles  3 1 1 4 2 0 1 6 0 5 6 1 5 0 2 0 0 0 4 1 4 0 2 2 10
```

This shows someone who collected 3 cans and 0 bottles.

(a) Which form deserves the prize for collecting cans?

(b) Which form deserves the prize for bottle collecting?
Explain your decision.

(c) Which form did better overall?
How did you decide?

A8 (a) Which team is working hardest?

(b) Which team has the easiest job?

Give reasons for your answers.

A

B

C

Mean tricks   a game for two to five players

You need a pack of playing cards without jacks, queens or kings.
Aces count as 1.

The object of the game is to use as many cards as
you can to get a target mean.

1 Decide how many rounds you will play.

Deal 7 cards each.

Turn over the top card from the ones that are left.

This is the target mean.

2 Each player then puts down cards whose mean is
the same as the target mean.

The number of cards you put down is your score.

(So the more the better!)

3 Keep a record of the scores.

The player with the highest total score wins.

Sue's cards

The target
mean is 6

Sue plays …

She scores 5

B Mean from frequencies

Here are the players in a football team.

70 kg 70 kg 70 kg 71 kg 71 kg 72 kg 72 kg 72 kg 72 kg 73 kg 73 kg

Here is a frequency table for the weights.

Weight in kg	Frequency
70	3
71	2
72	4
73	2

- How many players are there in the team?
  How do you get this from the numbers in
  the frequency table?

- There are three players who each weigh 70 kg.
  What is the total weight of these players?
  How do you get this from the numbers in the table?

- What is the total weight of those players who weigh 72 kg each?
  How do you get this from the table?

- What is the total weight of all the players in the team?
  Explain how you can get this from the numbers in the table.

- What is the mean weight of the players in the team?

B1 This table gives information about a rugby team.

(a) How many players weigh 78 kg?

(b) How many players are there altogether in the team?

(c) Calculate the total weight of all the players.

(d) Calculate the mean weight of the players, to 1 d.p.

Weight in kg	Frequency
75	2
76	4
77	2
78	5
79	2

B2 This data comes from a survey of birds' nests.
Calculate

(a) the number of nests surveyed

(b) the total number of eggs in all the nests

(c) the mean number of eggs per nest,
correct to 1 d.p.

Number of eggs in nest	Frequency
3	16
4	14
5	4

B3 Calculate the mean of this list of numbers.

How can you do it without having to add up every number separately?

| 3 | 3 | 3 | 3 | 4 | 4 | 4 | 4 | 4 | 4 | 4 | 4 | 5 | 5 | 5 | 5 | 5 | 6 |
| 6 | 6 | 6 | 7 | 7 | 7 | 8 | 8 | 8 | 8 | 8 | 8 | 8 | 9 | 9 | 9 | 9 | 9 |

B4 Jackie wants to find the mean number of goals scored by her favourite ice hockey team last season.

This is a frequency table of the goals scored.

(a) How many goals did they score altogether? Show how you found the answer.

(b) What was the mean number of goals scored by her team?

> This is the number of games.

Score	Tally	Frequency
0	⫫⫫	5
1	⫫⫫ ⫫⫫ //	12
2	⫫⫫ ⫫⫫ ///	13
3	⫫⫫ ///	8
4	//	2

B5 This frequency table gives information about Rashid's tomato plants.

Calculate the mean number of tomatoes on a plant.

Number of tomatoes	Tally	Frequency
4	⫫⫫ //	7
5	⫫⫫ ////	9
6	⫫⫫ ⫫⫫ /	11
7	⫫⫫ ⫫⫫	10
8	///	3
	Total	40

> This is the number of plants.

B6 Jon has fifteen tomato plants.
Two of them have 8 tomatoes each, three have 7 tomatoes each, nine have 6 tomatoes each and one has 5 tomatoes.

Calculate the mean number of tomatoes on a plant.

B7 This frequency bar chart gives information about the numbers of people in the cars passing a traffic census point.

Calculate the mean number of people in a car.

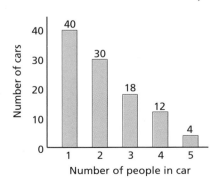

149

B8 Every time Marie went to the market, she kept a record of the price she paid for a cabbage.

Price in pence	57	58	59	60	61
Number of times paid	3	5	5	3	4

Find the mean price she paid.

B9 Leroy counted the number of Smarties in some tubes.

Number of Smarties in tube	26	28	29	30
Frequency	2	22	13	13

What was the mean number of Smarties in a tube?

B10 A firm that makes matches received a comment that the statement 'Average contents 50 matches' on a box of matches was misleading.

They counted the matches in many boxes. Here are their results.

Number of matches in box	48	49	50	51	52
Number of boxes	10	27	39	67	34

Find the mean number of matches per box.

Do you think the statement is misleading?

B11 Write down a list of five numbers.

(a) Find the mean of your set of numbers.

(b) What happens to the mean if you add 2 to each of the numbers in your list?

(c) Experiment with some other sets of numbers. What can you find out?

(d) Without using a calculator find the mean of   9761,   9763,   9760,   9762,   9764.

B12 Ms Rees's choir has fifty members.

Age in years	11	12	13	14	15	16
Number of boys	3	4	4	5	2	2
Number of girls	3	5	4	3	7	8

(a) What is the mean age of the boys?

(b) What is the mean age of the girls?

(c) What is the mean age of the choir?

Investigation

Investigate one of these statements.

'The mean sentence length is smaller in the *Mirror* than it is in the *Guardian*.'

'English words are shorter than German (or French) words.'

C Words

For pair or group work

At last she reached the end of the tunnel. It had been hard going lying on her back, holding tight to the plank and making her feet walk along the roof of the tunnel. It was not so much the exercise she minded, but the bits of brick and lime scale that continually fell from the roof onto her face and into her eyes. It was important to keep in time with the other legger as well: too fast and you did too much work, too slow meant you were making the other work too hard. It seemed like ages since she had entered _____ _____ _____ _____ _____ _____ _____ _____ _____ me
stood _____

The li_____ _____ _____ _____ _____ _____ most
welco_____ _____ _____ _____ the
residu_____ _____ _____ _____ _____ ndid
sundia_____ ning
but th_____ _____ st
decad_____ _____ ands
of mil_____ _____ utiful
canal_____

Usual_____ s. Yet
those _____ hard
men w_____ Cathy
went t_____ inted
barges_____ iron.
Coal w_____ pulling
the be_____

"Pull _____ spike
thrust_____ Red
blood _____ knee.
Uprigh_____ Three
bones _____

> This is a page from a story entered for a competition.
>
> The competition limit is 5000 words.
>
> C1 How could you estimate the number of words on this page of the story?
>
> Discuss your method and use it to make an estimate.
>
> C2 How many pages like this would come to 5000 words?

She wiped the lock key clean. It was never a pleasant scene when two barges travelling in opposite directions wanted to use the same lock. Time was money however, and with a sick parent waiting for her return at Birmingham it was essential that nobody held her up on the Grand Union canal today!

D Averages

What do you think these statements mean?

Mary is of average height.

The average maximum daily temperature in London in January is 7°C.

The average family uses about 400 litres of water a day.

This dot plot shows the weekly
pocket money of 11 young people.

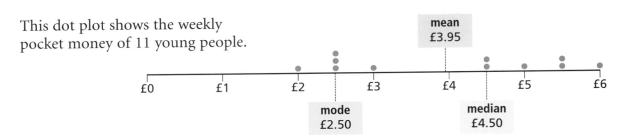

There are three kinds of average we can use.

Median The median (**£4.50**) is the middle value when the amounts are
arranged in order of size.

Mean To find the mean you add up the amounts and divide by
how many there are.

The mean is £43.50 ÷ 11 = **£3.95** (to the nearest penny).

Mode The mode is the amount which occurs most often (**£2.50**).

D1 Which average would you use if
  (a) you had £3 pocket money and thought you should have more
  (b) you were a parent of a child with £4.50 pocket money and
    thought they should have less

D2 These are the ages of the members of a swimming club.
  (a) Find the median, mean and modal ages.
  (b) Explain why the modal age is not a good
    representative value for the ages of this group.
  (c) Group people into ages 10–19, 20–29, etc.
    Find the modal age group.

13 17 19 24 15 39 49

34 25 34 18 20 25 16

44 21 37 18 15 13 22

54 18 20 38 26 17 46

24 33

D3 Averages are often used to compare sets of data.

Here are the hours of sunshine for the days of August in two seaside towns.

Blackmouth						
5	6	8	2	7	5	8
4	4	1	5	4	8	3
1	9	3	6	3	4	9
10	5	9	4	10	5	11
11	9	10				

Bournepool						
3	2	4	5	8	7	1
9	7	7	9	7	1	4
3	5	8	6	4	8	6
4	8	8	9	1	5	7
8	7	7				

Find the median, mean and modal number of hours of sunshine for each town. Compare the towns using averages.

E Mean challenges

E1 The mean weight of the players in a seven-a-side football team is 58 kg.
One player, who weighs 40 kg, is replaced by another, who weighs 54 kg.
What is the new mean weight of the team?

E2 The mean weight of the members of another seven-a-side team is 58 kg.
One member of the team, who weighs 43 kg, is replaced by another player.
The mean weight is now 60 kg.
What is the weight of the new player?

E3 The mean height of a group of four girls is 134 cm.
Another girl who is 140 cm tall joins the group.
What is the mean height now?

E4 Six girls, whose mean weight is 45 kg, join up with five boys, whose mean weight is 51 kg, to make a mixed football team.
What is the mean weight of the team?

E5 The oldest member of a family of five dies.
As a result, the mean age of the family goes down from 46 to 40.
How old was the person who died?

What progress have you made?

Statement

I can calculate the mean of a data set.

Evidence

1 The midday temperatures on the last seven days were (in °C) 14, 17, 13, 15, 12, 14, 9. Calculate the mean of these temperatures.

I can calculate the mean from a frequency table.

2 Raina surveyed birds' nests and got this data.

Number of eggs	0	1	2	3	4	5
Number of nests	2	4	3	6	8	2

Calculate the mean number of eggs per nest.

Review 2

1 Copy and complete each of these.

   (a) $5a + 20 = 5(............)$ (b) $6b - 12 = ...(b ....)$

   (c) $6c - 20 = ...(.........10)$ (d) $15d + 24 = ...(5d.........)$

2 (a) Round 437.9 to one significant figure.

   (b) Round 0.036 29 to two significant figures.

   (c) Round 8.0917 to two significant figures.

   (d) Estimate the answer to 28.37×0.0436 by rounding the numbers to one
      significant figure.

3 Work out the angles marked with letters.
  Give reasons.

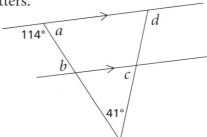

4 Alex, Bharat and Chris start a business and agree to share the profits
  so that Alex gets 45%, Bharat gets 36% and Chris gets the rest.

  In the first year the profits are £1290. How much does each person get?

5 Work out the input for each of these arrow diagrams.

   (a) 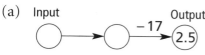   (b)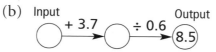

6 Suppose you have two identical
   right-angled triangles, cut out of
   card.

   This diagram shows how you
   can overlap the triangles so that
   the overlap is a square.

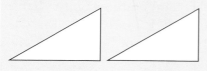

  Show how to overlap the two triangles so that the overlap is

  (a) a rhombus which is not a square   (b) a kite

  (c) a trapezium which is not a parallelogram

7 (a) I think of a number. I divide by 3, then add 10, then multiply by 5. The result is 75. What number did I think of?

(b) I think of a number. I subtract 7, then divide by 4, then add 9. The result is 12. What number did I think of?

8 Rajesh recorded the colour of each car in a car park. Here are his results.

Colour	Red	Blue	Green	White	Black	Other
Number of cars	11	9	4	8	3	2

(a) Calculate, to the nearest 1%, the percentage of cars that were of each colour.

(b) Draw a pie chart to show the information.

9 Which, if any, of the quadrilaterals shown here have

(a) one line of reflection symmetry and no rotation symmetry (other than order 1)

(b) two lines of reflection symmetry and rotation symmetry of order 2

(c) two lines of reflection symmetry and rotation symmetry of order 4

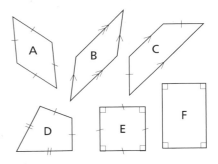

10 Simplify each of these expressions.

(a) $8 + 2x - 9 + x$ (b) $5 \times y \times 3y$ (c) $4p - 6 - 3p - 2$

11 Fiona recorded the number of people living in each house in her street. She summarised her results in this table.

Number in house	0	1	2	3	4	5	6
Frequency	2	3	7	9	6	4	3

Calculate the mean number of people per house, to one decimal place.

12 Given that $a = 7$, $b = {}^-8$ and $c = {}^-6$, evaluate each of these.

(a) $10 - 2a$ (b) $5 - 3b$ (c) $\frac{b}{2} + 3$ (d) $6 - \frac{c}{2}$ (e) $\frac{12 - b}{{}^-4}$

13 Work out the angles marked with letters. Give reasons.

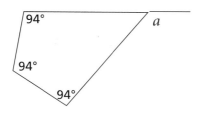
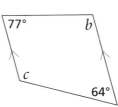
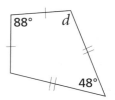

155

14 Is 551 is a prime number? If not, what is its prime factorisation?

15 Work out each of these angles. Give reasons.

   (a) angle FBC

   (b) angle GCD

   (c) angle BFC

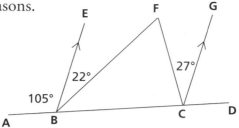

16 Copy and complete this table of equivalent fractions, decimals and percentages. Write each of the fractions in its simplest form.

Fraction	$\frac{4}{5}$				$\frac{17}{50}$		
Decimal		0.07		0.65			0.125
Percentage			48%			5%	

17 Gill is giving a children's party. She is not certain how many children will be coming. The number could be 3, 4, 5, 6 or 7.

She wants to buy some sweets so that whatever the number of children she will be able to share the sweets out equally.
What is the smallest number of sweets she needs?

18 Calculate the area of each of these shapes.

   (a)

                                (b)

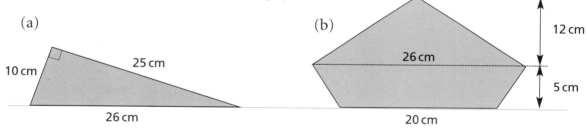

19 Draw these quadrilaterals accurately.

On your drawings measure the sides and angles not already given.

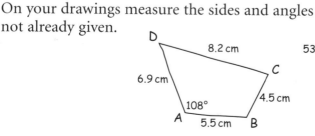

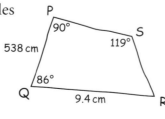

156

⑳ Know your calculator

This will help you

◆ use a calculator effectively
◆ evaluate expressions involving more than one operation
◆ substitute into formulas

A Order of operations

What results do you get from these sets of key presses?
Are they what you expected?

Ⓐ $\boxed{9} \boxed{-} \boxed{5} \boxed{-} \boxed{2}$ **Ⓑ** $\boxed{8} \boxed{\div} \boxed{4} \boxed{\div} \boxed{2}$ **Ⓒ** $\boxed{5} \boxed{+} \boxed{2} \boxed{\times} \boxed{3}$

Ⓓ $\boxed{9} \boxed{-} \boxed{6} \boxed{\div} \boxed{3}$ **Ⓔ** $\boxed{6} \boxed{\times} \boxed{4} \boxed{-} \boxed{1}$ **Ⓕ** $\boxed{6} \boxed{\div} \boxed{2} \boxed{+} \boxed{1}$

Ⓖ $\boxed{5} \boxed{-} \boxed{3} \boxed{+} \boxed{2}$ **Ⓗ** $\boxed{6} \boxed{\times} \boxed{9} \boxed{\div} \boxed{3}$ **Ⓘ** $\boxed{7} \boxed{+} \boxed{4} \boxed{\div} \boxed{2}$

Ⓙ $\boxed{8} \boxed{-} \boxed{3} \boxed{\times} \boxed{2}$ **Ⓚ** $\boxed{8} \boxed{\div} \boxed{2} \boxed{\times} \boxed{4}$

A1 Without using a calculator, evaluate these.

(a) $28 - 16 \div 4$ (b) $3 + 10 \times 3$ (c) $6 \times 7 + 1$ (d) $19 - 10 - 3$

(e) $15 - 5 \times 2$ (f) $36 \div 12 + 6$ (g) $4 \times 12 \div 3$ (h) $21 + 12 \div 3$

A2 Without using a calculator, find the missing number in each of these calculations.

(a) $20 - \blacksquare \times 2 = 10$ (b) $36 \div 3 + \blacksquare = 18$ (c) $\blacksquare - 45 \div 5 = 11$

(d) $3 \times \blacksquare - 6 = 24$ (e) $23 - \blacksquare + 2 = 15$ (f) $8 + 16 \div \blacksquare = 12$

(g) $\blacksquare \div 8 \div 2 = 2$ (h) $\blacksquare + 3 \times 3 = 21$ (i) $60 \div \blacksquare \div 6 = 2$

A3 In the expression below, you can replace each diamond with $+$, $-$, $\times$ or $\div$.

24 ◊ 8 ◊ 2   (For example, you could make $24 \div 8 + 2 = 5$.)

You must not use brackets or change the order of the numbers.

Show how to make the result   (a) 190   (b) 28   (c) 8   (d) 1.5

B Brackets

Always evaluate expressions in brackets first.

$$2 \times (3 + 4)$$
$$= 2 \times 7$$
$$= 14$$

If there are no brackets, then
- *multiply or divide before you add or subtract*
- *otherwise, work from left to right*

$$3 + 4 \times 2$$
$$= 3 + 8$$
$$= 11$$

B1 Without using a calculator, evaluate these.

(a) $5 \times (10 - 3)$ (b) $5 \times 10 - 3$ (c) $(9 + 6) \div 3$ (d) $9 + 6 \div 3$

(e) $20 \div (5 - 1)$ (f) $20 \div 5 - 1$ (g) $12 - (6 + 1)$ (h) $12 - 6 + 1$

B2 Find the missing number in each of these calculations.

(a) $(16 - \blacksquare) \times 2 = 10$ (b) $16 - \blacksquare \times 2 = 10$ (c) $\blacksquare + 5 \times 2 = 16$

(d) $(\blacksquare + 5) \times 2 = 16$ (e) $12 - (\blacksquare - 1) = 2$ (f) $12 - \blacksquare - 1 = 2$

(g) $24 \div 4 + \blacksquare = 8$ (h) $24 \div (4 + \blacksquare) = 8$ (i) $13 - \blacksquare \div 3 = 4$

B3 The expression $36 + (6 \times 2)$ has the same value as $36 + 6 \times 2$, so brackets are not needed.

Do these expressions need brackets? Write 'yes' or 'no' for each one.

(a) $36 + (6 - 2)$ (b) $(36 + 6) \times 2$ (c) $36 - (6 \div 2)$ (d) $(36 - 6) \div 2$

(e) $(36 \times 6) - 2$ (f) $36 \div (6 \div 2)$ (g) $(36 \div 6) + 2$ (h) $36 - (6 - 2)$

(i) $36 \times (6 \times 2)$ (j) $(36 \div 6) - 2$ (k) $36 \div (6 - 2)$ (l) $36 \times (6 \div 2)$

C A thin dividing line

For division we can use a horizontal line.

$$6 + 4 \div 2 = 6 + \frac{4}{2} \qquad (6 + 4) \div 2 = \frac{6 + 4}{2} \qquad 6 \div 4 + 2 = \frac{6}{4} + 2 \qquad 6 \div (4 + 2) = \frac{6}{4 + 2}$$

C1 Find four matching pairs of expressions.

A $(20 - 4) \div 2$ **B** $20 - \frac{4}{2}$ **C** $\frac{20 - 4}{2}$ **D** $\frac{20}{4 - 2}$ **E** $\frac{20}{2} - 4$

F $20 \div (4 - 2)$ **G** $20 - 4 \div 2$ **H** $20 \div 4 - 2$ **I** $\frac{20}{4} - 2$

C2 Write these expressions using a line to show division.

(a) $60 + 3 \div 2$ (b) $(23 - 7) \div 4$ (c) $(100 + 5) \div 3$ (d) $4 - 6 \div 5$

(e) $5 \div (3 - 1)$ (f) $18 \div 9 - 1$ (g) $4 + 12 \div (5 - 2)$

C3 Evaluate these without a calculator.

(a) $\dfrac{20 - 6}{2}$ (b) $10 + \dfrac{5}{2}$ (c) $\dfrac{32}{4} - 7$ (d) $\dfrac{36}{12 - 3}$

(e) $\dfrac{19 + 6}{5}$ (f) $\dfrac{4 + 6 \times 2}{8}$ (g) $\dfrac{14 + 7}{5 - 2}$ (h) $5 + \dfrac{50}{2 + 8}$

C4 You can find the value of $\dfrac{9 - 3}{2}$ with these key presses: $\boxed{(}\ \boxed{9}\ \boxed{-}\ \boxed{3}\ \boxed{)}\ \boxed{\div}\ \boxed{2}$

Using brackets keys where necessary, use your calculator to evaluate these.

(a) $\dfrac{16 + 24}{8}$ (b) $\dfrac{14}{7} + 3$ (c) $\dfrac{28}{14 - 10}$ (d) $8 + \dfrac{108}{4}$ (e) $\dfrac{11 + 6}{3.4}$

C5 Predict the result your calculator will give for each of these sets of key presses. Then check with the calculator.

(a) $\boxed{(}\ \boxed{8}\ \boxed{+}\ \boxed{4}\ \boxed{)}\ \boxed{\div}\ \boxed{(}\ \boxed{2}\ \boxed{+}\ \boxed{1}\ \boxed{)}$

(b) $\boxed{(}\ \boxed{8}\ \boxed{+}\ \boxed{4}\ \boxed{)}\ \boxed{\div}\ \boxed{2}\ \boxed{+}\ \boxed{1}$

C6 Evaluate   (a) $\dfrac{16 + 14}{5} - 4.5$ (b) $\dfrac{16 + 14}{5 - 4.5}$ (c) $\dfrac{7 + 3 \times 6}{8 - 3}$

C7 (a) Find the result of each set of key presses below.

(i) $\boxed{4}\ \boxed{+}\ \boxed{5}\ \boxed{\times}\ \boxed{3}$ (ii) $\boxed{4}\ \boxed{+}\ \boxed{5}\ \boxed{=}\ \boxed{\times}\ \boxed{3}$

(iii) $\boxed{6}\ \boxed{+}\ \boxed{9}\ \boxed{\div}\ \boxed{3}$ (iv) $\boxed{6}\ \boxed{+}\ \boxed{9}\ \boxed{=}\ \boxed{\div}\ \boxed{3}$

(b) Describe the effect of using the $\boxed{=}$ key in the middle of a calculation.

C8 For each set of key presses below, predict the result your calculator will give. Then check with the calculator.

(a) $\boxed{8}\ \boxed{-}\ \boxed{1}\ \boxed{=}\ \boxed{\times}\ \boxed{3}$ (b) $\boxed{3}\ \boxed{+}\ \boxed{7}\ \boxed{=}\ \boxed{\div}\ \boxed{2}$

(c) $\boxed{1}\ \boxed{8}\ \boxed{-}\ \boxed{3}\ \boxed{\times}\ \boxed{2}\ \boxed{=}\ \boxed{\div}\ \boxed{6}$

C9 Which of these could you use to evaluate $\dfrac{9 + 1}{5}$?

A $\boxed{9}\ \boxed{+}\ \boxed{1}\ \boxed{=}\ \boxed{\div}\ \boxed{5}$ **B** $\boxed{9}\ \boxed{+}\ \boxed{1}\ \boxed{\div}\ \boxed{5}$ **C** $\boxed{(}\ \boxed{9}\ \boxed{+}\ \boxed{1}\ \boxed{)}\ \boxed{\div}\ \boxed{5}$

C10 Write down a set of key presses you could use to evaluate $\dfrac{7 - 1}{2 + 1}$.

D Complex calculations

The calculator's **memory** can be used to store the result of a calculation for future use.

The key which puts the displayed number into the memory may be labelled
M in or **Store**.
The key which displays the number currently in the memory may be **M out** or **Recall**.

The memory can be used instead of brackets.
For example, $9 \div (5 - 2)$ can be done like this:

D1 Use the memory to evaluate each of these.

(a) $2.7 \times (0.85 + 6.42)$ (b) $\dfrac{13.6}{8.5 - 2.1}$ (c) $\dfrac{11.3 + 14.2}{3.2 - 1.7}$ (d) $15.8 - \dfrac{24.3}{6.3 - 1.8}$

D2 Evaluate each of these expressions using either brackets keys or the memory.

(a) $\dfrac{63.9 - 23.4}{3.6}$ (b) $\dfrac{2.8 + 9.8}{1.4}$ (c) $\dfrac{9.25}{6.1 - 2.4}$

(d) $(3.1 + 5.4) \times 2.6$ (e) $\dfrac{11 - 1.5}{1.76 + 0.74}$ (f) $\dfrac{1.9 + 1.3}{16 \times 0.4}$

(g) $\dfrac{1.3 \times 3.6}{2 - 0.8}$ (h) $3 \times \dfrac{41.4 - 32.2}{9.2}$ (i) $\dfrac{(6.3 + 9.2) \times 0.4}{0.2}$

E Squares

To calculate with squares, evaluate expressions in brackets first,
and square before you multiply, divide, add or subtract.

$(10 - 3)^2$	$10 - 3^2$	4×3^2	$(4 \times 3)^2$
$= 7^2$	$= 10 - 9$	$= 4 \times 9$	$= 12^2$
$= 49$	$= 1$	$= 36$	$= 144$

E1 Without using a calculator, evaluate these.

(a) $(2 + 3)^2$ (b) 2×5^2 (c) $10 + 2 \times 4^2$ (d) $5 \times 3^2 - 20$

(e) $(3 \times 4)^2 + 1$ (f) $\dfrac{6^2}{3}$ (g) $\dfrac{32}{4^2}$ (h) $\dfrac{6^2}{12 - 3}$

E2 Predict the result of each set of key presses below and then check with a calculator.

(a) $\boxed{4}\ \boxed{\times}\ \boxed{5}\ \boxed{x^2}$ (b) $\boxed{(}\ \boxed{4}\ \boxed{\times}\ \boxed{5}\ \boxed{)}\ \boxed{x^2}$ (c) $\boxed{1}\ \boxed{8}\ \boxed{\div}\ \boxed{3}\ \boxed{x^2}$

(d) $\boxed{(}\ \boxed{1}\ \boxed{5}\ \boxed{\div}\ \boxed{5}\ \boxed{)}\ \boxed{x^2}$ (e) $\boxed{6}\ \boxed{+}\ \boxed{4}\ \boxed{x^2}\ \boxed{\div}\ \boxed{8}$

E3 Write down a set of key presses you could use to evaluate these.

(a) 5×7^2 (b) $(5 + 7)^2$ (c) $\dfrac{100}{5^2}$

E4 For each set of key presses below, predict the result and then check it.

(a) $\boxed{2}\,\boxed{\times}\,\boxed{6}\,\boxed{x^2}$ (b) $\boxed{1}\,\boxed{0}\,\boxed{-}\,\boxed{3}\,\boxed{x^2}$ (c) $\boxed{(}\,\boxed{7}\,\boxed{+}\,\boxed{2}\,\boxed{)}\,\boxed{x^2}$

(d) $\boxed{4}\,\boxed{x^2}\,\boxed{\div}\,\boxed{(}\,\boxed{2}\,\boxed{+}\,\boxed{6}\,\boxed{)}$ (e) $\boxed{4}\,\boxed{x^2}\,\boxed{\div}\,\boxed{2}\,\boxed{+}\,\boxed{6}$

(f) $\boxed{3}\,\boxed{6}\,\boxed{-}\,\boxed{2}\,\boxed{7}\,\boxed{\div}\,\boxed{3}\,\boxed{x^2}$ (g) $\boxed{8}\,\boxed{+}\,\boxed{6}\,\boxed{\div}\,\boxed{2}\,\boxed{x^2}\,\boxed{-}\,\boxed{3}$

E5 Which sets of key presses below could you use to evaluate $\dfrac{21 - 3^2}{3 - 1}$?

A $\boxed{(}\,\boxed{2}\,\boxed{1}\,\boxed{-}\,\boxed{3}\,\boxed{x^2}\,\boxed{)}\,\boxed{\div}\,\boxed{3}\,\boxed{-}\,\boxed{1}$

B $\boxed{(}\,\boxed{2}\,\boxed{1}\,\boxed{-}\,\boxed{3}\,\boxed{x^2}\,\boxed{)}\,\boxed{\div}\,\boxed{(}\,\boxed{3}\,\boxed{-}\,\boxed{1}\,\boxed{)}$

C $\boxed{2}\,\boxed{1}\,\boxed{-}\,\boxed{3}\,\boxed{x^2}\,\boxed{\div}\,\boxed{(}\,\boxed{3}\,\boxed{-}\,\boxed{1}\,\boxed{)}$

D $\boxed{2}\,\boxed{1}\,\boxed{-}\,\boxed{3}\,\boxed{x^2}\,\boxed{=}\,\boxed{\div}\,\boxed{(}\,\boxed{3}\,\boxed{-}\,\boxed{1}\,\boxed{)}$

E $\boxed{3}\,\boxed{-}\,\boxed{1}\,\boxed{\substack{M\\in}}\,\boxed{2}\,\boxed{1}\,\boxed{-}\,\boxed{3}\,\boxed{x^2}\,\boxed{=}\,\boxed{\div}\,\boxed{\substack{M\\out}}$

E6 Write down a set of key presses you could use to evaluate $\dfrac{15 + 9^2}{4^2}$.

E7 Evaluate these expressions.

(a) $(3.6 - 1.2)^2$ (b) 0.2×5^2 (c) $\dfrac{4.2 + 0.3^2}{2.86}$

(d) $\dfrac{2.4 \times 9^2}{5.4}$ (e) $\dfrac{(1.5 \times 6)^2}{3.5 - 2.6}$ (f) $10 - \dfrac{3.2^2}{4}$

(g) $\dfrac{6.5 + 3.1^2}{3 \times 1.79}$ (h) $\dfrac{(1.81 + 2.7^2) \times 3}{2.6}$ (i) $\dfrac{8.6 + 3.1 \times 9^2}{7^2 - 24}$

E8 Arrange these cards in a line so that the result has the highest possible value.

$\boxed{3}\ \boxed{4}\ \boxed{5}\ \boxed{6}\ \boxed{2}\ \boxed{+}\ \boxed{\times}\ \boxed{\div}$

F Square roots

The square root operation $\sqrt{\ }$, like squaring, takes precedence over $\times, \div, +, -$.
On some calculators the square root key is pressed after the number.

$\sqrt{16} + 9$
$= 4 + 9$
$= 13$

F1 Work these out.

(a) $\sqrt{(9 + 16)}$ (b) $\sqrt{9} + 16$ (c) $\sqrt{9} \times 16$ (d) $\dfrac{4 \times \sqrt{100} - 12}{\sqrt{25} + 9}$

F2 Evaluate each of these expressions.

(a) $\sqrt{(23.15 - 10.9)}$ (b) $\sqrt{17.64} + 7.36$ (c) $1.25 + \sqrt{10.89} \times 1.44$

(d) $\dfrac{13.52 + 10.91}{\sqrt{8.41} + 0.59}$ (e) $24.7 - \dfrac{10.2}{\sqrt{2.89}}$ (f) $\dfrac{\sqrt{7.29} + 1.71}{0.34 - 0.18}$

F3 Arrange these cards $\boxed{1}\,\boxed{4}\,\boxed{9}\,\boxed{\sqrt{\ }}\,\boxed{+}\,\boxed{\div}$ in a line so that the result is

(a) 11   (b) 13   (c) 5.5   (d) 3.25   (e) 1.75   (f) 9.5

G Negative numbers

The 'change sign' key, usually labelled (–) or +/–, changes a positive number to
a negative, and a negative to a positive.

On some calculators the change sign key is pressed after the number.

G1 Find out how to do each of these calculations on your calculator

$^-8 + 2$ $8 - ^-2$ $6 + ^-9$ $^-3 + ^-7$ $^-3 - ^-7$ $^-4 \times ^-3$

Check that the results are what you expect.

G2 Evaluate these.

(a) $\dfrac{^-12.7 + 7.9}{1.28}$ (b) $^-10.4 - \dfrac{2.89}{3.4}$ (c) $\dfrac{2.68}{1.45 - ^-1.75}$ (d) $^-6.6 + \dfrac{3.18}{2.33 - 4.45}$

G3 The length of this metal rod depends on
its temperature.

L cm

The length, L cm, at temperature T°C is given by the formula

$L = 60.2(1 + 0.0002T)$

Calculate L to one decimal place when T is   (a) 325°C   (b) $^-48$°C

G4 Copy and complete the cross-number puzzle.

Across

1 $\dfrac{26^2 - 76}{4^2 - 10} + 5$

4 $\dfrac{^-40 + 32^2}{3}$

5 $(^-2 \times {}^-11)^2 - 8$

7 $\left(\dfrac{^-126}{^-9}\right)^2 + 2$

Down

1 $\dfrac{^-13 \times 16^2 + 62^2}{3 + 4 \times 10}$

2 $(99 - {}^-12 \times 11)^2$

3 $\dfrac{12^2}{48} + \dfrac{8^2 - 1}{3^2} + 8$

5 $2 \times 5^2 - 1$

6 $3 + \dfrac{45^2}{27}$

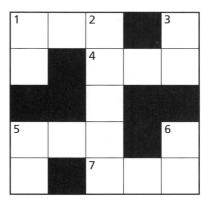

What progress have you made?

Statement	Evidence

Statement

I can evaluate expressions involving more than one operation without a calculator.

Evidence

1 Evaluate these.

(a) $7 + 8 \times 4$ (b) $42 - \dfrac{28}{7}$

(c) $11 - 3^2$ (d) $\sqrt{25} \times 4 - 19$

Statement

I can use a calculator to evaluate expressions involving more than one operation.

Evidence

2 Evaluate these.

(a) $8.7 + 6.5 \times 3.8$ (b) $13 + \dfrac{13}{2.6}$

(c) $\dfrac{5.54 - 2.19}{4.82 + 1.58}$ (d) $\dfrac{3.8 + 6.7}{0.6 \times 3.5}$

Statement

I can use the square and square root keys.

Evidence

3 Evaluate these.

(a) $6.6 + 4.6^2$ (b) $\dfrac{9.82 + \sqrt{2.89}}{1.19 + 1.37}$

Statement

I can deal with negative numbers on a calculator.

Evidence

4 Evaluate these.

(a) $^-1.7 - 3.9 \times {}^-6.6$

(b) $\dfrac{8.75 - {}^-1.49}{^-0.8 \times 2.56}$

21 Three dimensions

This work will help you

- ◆ describe, make and draw 3-D objects
- ◆ find the volumes of cuboids and prisms
- ◆ draw nets and find the surface areas of 3-D objects

A Drawing three-dimensional objects

This object is made with four cubes.

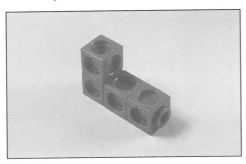

Here is a drawing of the object.

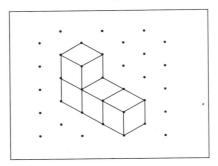

- There are 8 possible objects you can make with four cubes.
  Can you make and draw them all?

- Can you imagine the different shapes that can be made with five cubes?
  Try to sketch them on triangular dotty paper without making them.

B Views

Three people are looking at a shape.

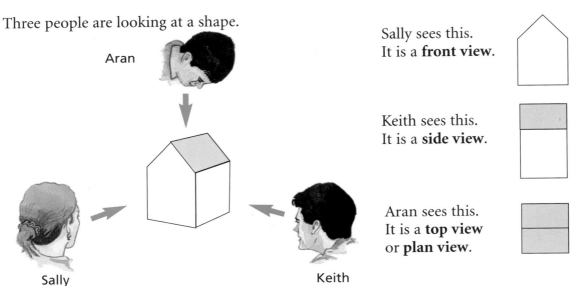

Aran

Sally

Keith

Sally sees this.
It is a **front view**.

Keith sees this.
It is a **side view**.

Aran sees this.
It is a **top view**
or **plan view**.

B1 This shape is made with five cubes.
This is the front view of the shape.

(a) Draw the side view.

(b) Draw the top view.

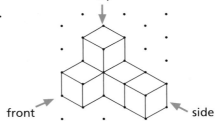

B2 Draw a front, side and top view of each of these shapes.
Label the views clearly.

(a)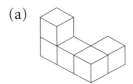

(b)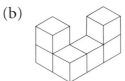

(c)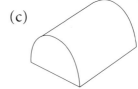

B3 Four views of a model building are
drawn below.

(a) Match each view to one of
the directions shown by arrows.

(b) The view from one direction is missing.
Draw this view.

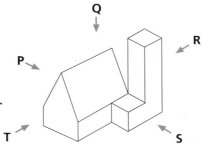

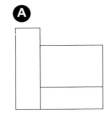

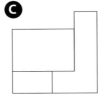

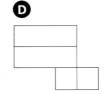

B4 These are views of some everyday objects.
For each object there are two views, which may be front, side or top.
Identify the objects and sketch the missing view of each one.

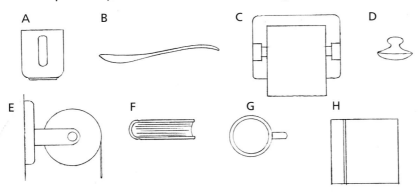

C Volume of a cuboid

The volume of a 3-D object is how much space it takes up.
A cube 1 cm by 1 cm by 1 cm has a volume of **1 cm³**.
Volumes are often measured in cm³.

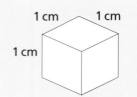

C1 These shapes are cuboids.
Find the volume of each one.

(a)

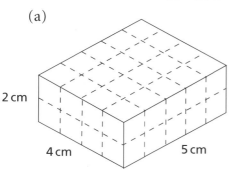

(b)

(c)

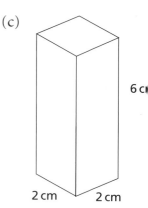

C2 Find the volume of each of these cuboids.
- (a) 3 cm by 2 cm by 5 cm
- (b) 2 cm by 4 cm by 6 cm
- (c) 1 cm by 4 cm by 7 cm
- (d) 3 cm by 3 cm by 4 cm

To find the volume of a cuboid, just multiply length × width × height.

C3 Calculate the volume of this cuboid.
Explain how you can see by counting cubes that
the result is correct.

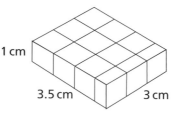

C4 Calculate the volume of this cuboid.
Check by counting cubes.

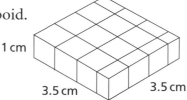

C5 Find the volume of each of these cuboids.
- (a) 2 cm by 4 cm by 4.5 cm
- (b) 2.5 cm by 6 cm by 3 cm
- (c) 2.5 cm by 3.5 cm by 8 cm
- (d) 4.5 cm by 3 cm by 1.5 cm

C6 All of these cuboids have the same volume.
Find the missing measurements. (The diagrams are not all drawn to the same scale!)

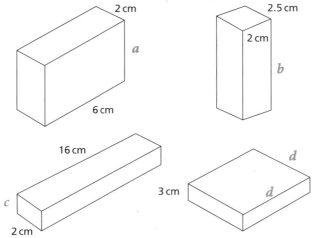
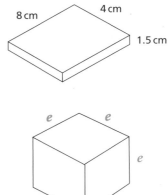

C7 'Whoosh' washing powder is packed in boxes 8 cm by 15 cm by 20 cm.

The makers need to make a box which has exactly twice the volume.

What possible measurements could they use for the new box?

Cubic metres

Large volumes are measured in cubic metres (m^3).

A cube with edges 1 m has a volume of $1\,m^3$.

- How many pupils could get into this cubic metre?
- Roughly what is the volume of your classroom in m^3?

Believe it or not ...

In 1987 a giant iceberg, called B-9, broke away from the mainland of Antarctica.

It was roughly a cuboid 154 km long, 35 km wide and 250 m deep.

What was its volume?

D Prisms

All of the shapes below are prisms.

What is a prism?

These shapes are prisms...

... but these are not.

E Volume of a prism

A prism with cross-sectional area 1 cm² and length 4 cm has a volume of 4 cm³.

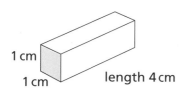

1 cm

1 cm

length 4 cm

A shape made up of six such prisms will have a volume of
$6 \times 4 \, cm^3 = 24 \, cm^3$.

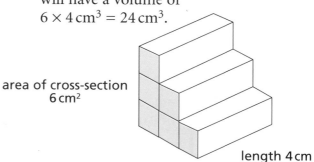

area of cross-section
6 cm²

length 4 cm

Volume of prism = area of cross-section × length

E1 Find the volume of each of these prisms.
They are all made from centimetre cubes (or parts of them).

(a)

(b)

(c)

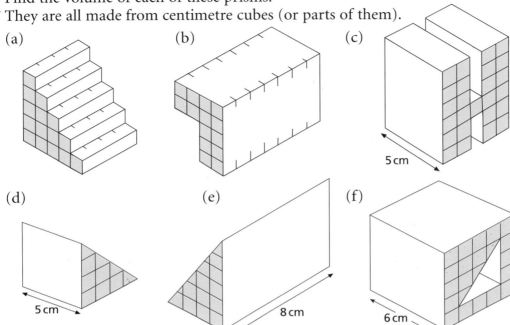

(d)

5 cm

(e)

8 cm

(f)

6 cm

E2 Calculate the volume of each of these prisms.

(a)

5 cm   3 cm   1 cm
4 cm   6 cm

(b)

6 cm   4 cm
2 cm
3 cm
2 cm

(c)

1 cm
6 cm   4 cm
7 cm
5 cm

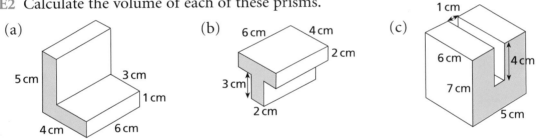

E3 Calculate the volume of each of these prisms.

(a)

4 cm
5 cm   6 cm

(b)

3 cm   7 cm
9 cm

(c)

6 cm
10 cm
6 cm

(d)

3 cm   5 cm
8 cm

(e)

5 cm
4 cm
4.5 cm
7 cm

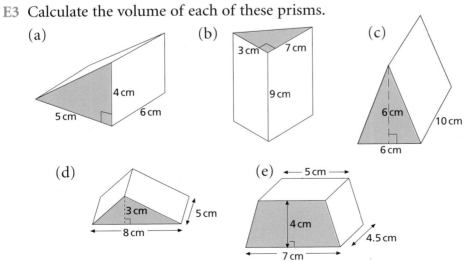

169

E4 A garden pond has an area of 6.2 m².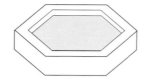
It is 0.45 m deep at all points.

What is the volume of the pond?

E5 Mr and Mrs Windsor are building a shed.
The shed will stand on a concrete base whose area is 14.5 m².
They buy 8 m³ of ready mixed concrete to make the base.

How thick will the base be? Give your answer to a sensible degree of accuracy.

E6 A block of copper with volume 1 cm³ is rolled out to make wire.
The wire must have cross-sectional area 0.025 cm².

How long will the wire be?

E7 A block of steel is 20 cm by 10 cm by 10 cm.
It is rolled into a sheet which is 0.5 cm thick.

What will be the area of the sheet?

E8 If 8 m³ of sand is spread to a depth of 20 cm, what area will it cover?

E9 Sketch two different prisms which both have a volume 480 cm³.
Show all the dimensions of your prisms.

E10 A prism has volume 100 cm³.
The height of the prism is 5 cm.

Sketch three prisms this could be. Show all the dimensions.

E11 What happens to the volume of a cuboid if

(a) one dimension is doubled

(b) two dimensions are doubled

(c) all three dimensions are doubled

*E12 The height of a cuboid is double the width.
The length is three times the width.
The volume is 2058 cm³.

What are the dimensions of this cuboid?

*E13 The length and the width of this prism
and the height of its triangular end are all equal.
The volume is 665.5 cm³.

What is the length?

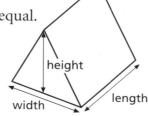

F Nets

A flat shape which can be folded up to make a three-dimensional shape is called a **net** of the three-dimensional shape.

Here are three nets, P, Q and R.

Sketch the three-dimensional shape which you would make with each net.

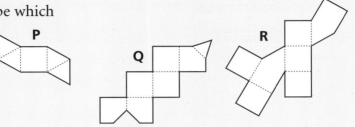

F1 (a) The shaded shape is an incomplete net of a cuboid.
The dotted line shows one possible position for the missing face.
Copy the diagram and show all the other possible positions for the missing face.

(b) Copy this incomplete net and show all the possible positions for the missing face.

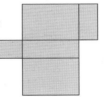

F2 (a) Is each of these a net of a cube?

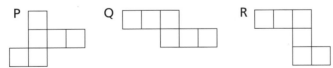

(b) How many different nets of a cube can you find?

F3 This cube has a cross on the bottom and an arrow on each of the four vertical faces.
All the arrows point to the left.
Copy and complete these two nets of the cube showing the cross, and all the arrows pointing the correct way.

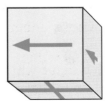

(a)

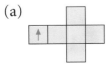

(b)

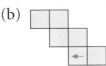

F4 (a) The blue line on this net makes one continuous loop when the net is folded to make a cube.
Sketch the cube.

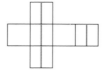

(b) Copy and complete this net so that a blue line makes a different continuous loop on the cube.
Sketch the cube.

F5 Here are the nets of some three-dimensional shapes.
Sketch each shape and write its name if you know it.

(a)

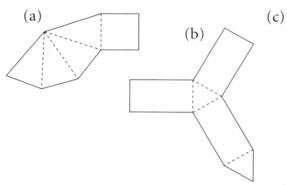

(b)

(c)

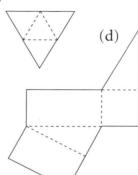

(d)

(e)

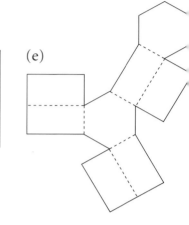

F6 The top and bottom of a box are identical quarter-circles.

(a) Copy and complete this sketch of a shape which could be folded up to make the box.

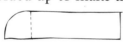

(b) Sketch a different shape which could be folded up to make the box.

F7 The ends of this box are semi-circles.
Sketch a shape which could be folded up to make the box.

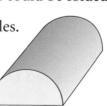

F8 Sketch a shape which could be folded up to make this box.

G Surface area

The **surface area** of a solid is the total area of all its faces …

… which is the same as the area of its net.

 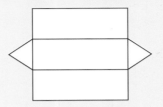

G1 Here is the net of a cuboid.

What is the surface area of the cuboid?

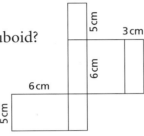

G2 What is the surface area of each of these cuboids?

(a) 4 cm by 3 cm by 7 cm

(b) 9 cm by 4 cm by 5 cm

(c) 2.5 cm by 4.5 cm by 8 cm

(d) 1.5 cm by 2.5 cm by 3.5 cm

G3 Do cuboids with the same volume have the same surface area?
Give examples to show how you came to your conclusion.

G4 The volume of this cuboid is 144 cm³.

What is its surface area?

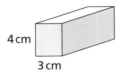

G5 The volume of a cuboid is 195 cm³.
The lengths of two edges are 2.5 cm and 12 cm.
Calculate the surface area.

G6 The surface area of this cuboid is 332 cm².

What is its height?

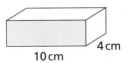

G7 The surface area of a cuboid is 76 cm².
Two edges are of lengths 4 cm and 8 cm.
Calculate the volume of the cuboid.

What progress have you made?

Statement	Evidence

I can draw three-dimensional objects on dotty paper.

1 Make an object with five cubes and draw it.

2 Draw three views of this object.

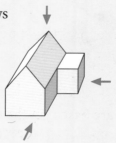

I can find the volume of a cuboid.

3 Find the volume of a cuboid 5 cm by 4 cm by 1.5 cm.

I can calculate the volume of a prism.

4 Find the volume of this prism.

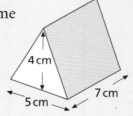

I can calculate the length of a prism given the volume and cross-sectional area.

5 $5 \, m^3$ of concrete is to be spread over a floor with area $12 \, m^2$. How thick will it be?

I can draw the net of a solid.

6 Sketch a net for each of these.

(a) 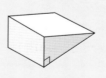 (b)

I can find the surface area of a cuboid.

7 Find the surface area of a cuboid 5 cm by 4 cm by 1.5 cm.

22 Finding formulas

This work will help you
- ◆ find a formula from a geometric expression
- ◆ find a formula for a linear sequence

A Maori patterns

For class discussion

Some of the geometric patterns in this work are based on the weaving and stitching patterns used by Maoris in New Zealand.

The Maori women in this photo are weaving flax strips through wooden slats.

These *tukutuku* panels are then used to decorate the walls of the Maori great houses.

An example of Maori patterns	Pattern 1	Pattern 2	Pattern 3
	××× ×	××××× × ×	××××××× × × ×

A1 Look at the patterns on the right.

(a) Sketch pattern 4 and pattern 5.

(b) Explain what pattern 10 would look like.

Pattern 1   Pattern 2   Pattern 3

(c) Copy and complete this table.

Pattern number	1	2	3	4	5
Number of crosses					

(d) How many crosses will there be in
(i) pattern 10   (ii) pattern 50   (iii) pattern 100

(e) How many crosses are there in pattern n?

A2 (a) Sketch pattern 4 and pattern 5.

(b) Explain what pattern 10 would look like.

(c) Work out how many crosses there would be in pattern 100.

(d) Find a formula for the number of crosses in the nth pattern.

(e) One of these patterns has 56 crosses. Which one is it?

Pattern 1   Pattern 2   Pattern 3

A3 This Maori design is called *tapatoru*.

(a) Sketch pattern 3 and pattern 5.

(b) How many crosses would there be in pattern 100?

(c) How many crosses are there in the nth pattern?

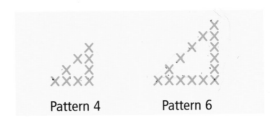

Pattern 4   Pattern 6

A4 (a) Sketch pattern 2 and pattern 4.

(b) Explain what pattern 10 would look like.

(c) How many crosses would there be in pattern 100?

(d) How many crosses are there in the nth pattern?

(e) One of these patterns has 84 crosses. Which one is it?

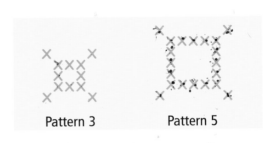

Pattern 3   Pattern 5

A5 (a) Sketch pattern 2 and pattern 4.

(b) Explain what pattern 10 would look like.

(c) How many crosses would there be in pattern 100?

(d) How many crosses are there in the nth pattern?

(e) One of these patterns has 229 crosses. Which one is it?

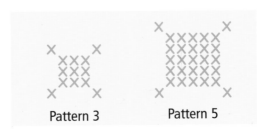

Pattern 3   Pattern 5

*A6 Find a formula for the number of crosses in the *n*th pattern.

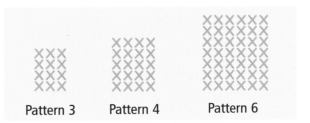

Pattern 3   Pattern 4   Pattern 6

A7 On squared paper, invent a weaving design of your own.

Draw some of the patterns and find a formula for the number of crosses in the *n*th pattern.

B Matchstick patterns

Find a formula for the number of matches in the *n*th pattern.

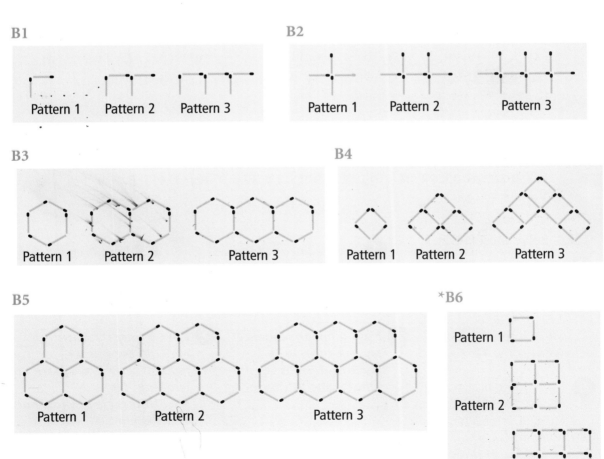

B1

Pattern 1   Pattern 2   Pattern 3

B2

Pattern 1   Pattern 2   Pattern 3

B3

Pattern 1   Pattern 2   Pattern 3

B4

Pattern 1   Pattern 2   Pattern 3

B5

Pattern 1   Pattern 2   Pattern 3

*B6

Pattern 1

Pattern 2

Pattern 3

C Sequences

What different ways can you think of to continue these sequences?

1, 2, 4, ... ?

2, 4, 6, ... ?

The numbers in a sequence are called **terms** of the sequence.

C1 This is the sequence of **triangle numbers**.

1   3   6   10   15   ...

(a) Describe the rule to go from one term to the next.

(b) Use your rule to find the 7th term.

C2 For each of the following sequences,

(i) describe a rule to go from one term to the next   (ii) find the 8th term

(a) 9, 14, 19, 24, 29, ...   (b) 2, 3, 6, 11, 18, ...   (c) 1, 3, 7, 15, 31, ...

(d) $3, 2\frac{3}{4}, 2\frac{1}{2}, 2\frac{1}{4}, 2, ...$ (e) 3, 6, 12, 24, 48, ...   (f) 1, 3, 4, 7, 11, ...

Linear sequences go up or down in equal steps.

C3 Is each of these sequences linear or non-linear?

(a) 4, 10, 16, 22, 28, 34   (b) 3, 6, 9, 15, 24, 39   (c) 3, 4, 5, 6, 7, 9, 12

(d) 7, 4, 1, ⁻2, ⁻5, ⁻8   (e) 3, 3.2, 3.4, 3.6, 3.8, 4

C4 Solve these puzzles.

1 I am a linear sequence.
My differences are 6, 6, 6, ...
My second term is 1.
What is my 10th term?

2 I am a linear sequence.
My 3rd term is 5.
My 9th term is 29.
What is my 6th term?

3 I am a non-linear sequence.
My differences are 1, 2, 3, 4, 5, 6, ...
My 4th term is 13.
What is my 1st term?

4 I am a linear sequence.
My 4th term is 36.
My 20th term is 12.
What is my 8th term?

5 I am a linear sequence.
My 10th term is 44.
My 2nd term is a square number less than 10.
My 5th term is a whole number.
What is my 11th term?

6 I am a linear sequence.
My 1st term is less than 0.
My 2nd term is a square number.
My 4th term is a cube number with one digit.
What is my 6th term?

7 I am a linear sequence. My 1st term is less than 10.
My first five terms are prime numbers less than 30.
What is my 7th term?

178

D Sequences from rules

One way to describe a sequence is to give a formula for the nth term.

This table shows the first few terms of the sequence whose nth term is $2n + 9$.

Term number (n)	1	2	3	4	5	6	...
Terms of the sequence ($2n + 9$)	11	13	15	17	19	21	...

The difference is 2 each time, so this is a linear sequence.

D1 The nth term of a sequence is $3n - 2$.

(a) Write down the first five terms of the sequence.

(b) What are the differences for this sequence? Is it a linear sequence?

D2 Match each sequence to a correct expression for its nth term.

(a) 6, 10, 14, 18, 22, ...   (b) 5, 6, 7, 8, 9, ...   (c) ⁻3, 2, 7, 12, 17, ...

(d) 0, 3, 8, 15, 24, ...   (e) 5, 13, 21, 29, 37, ...

$n + 4$ ⁻ $n^2 - 1$ $5n - 8$ · $4n + 2$ $n + 1$ · $8n - 3$ ·

D3 Each expression below gives the nth term of a sequence.

For each expression   (i)   find the first six terms of the sequence

(ii) decide if the sequence is linear

(iii) work out the 100th term of the sequence

(a) $5n$ (b) $5n + 1$ (c) $4n$ (d) $4n - 3$ (e) $3n - 9$

(f) n^2 (g) $50 - n$ (h) $n^2 + 1$ (i) $30 - 2n$ (j) $\dfrac{12}{n}$

E Finding a formula for a linear sequence

Can you find a formula for the nth term of each of these sequences?

A

Term number (n)	1	2	3	4	5	6	...
Sequence	3	6	9	12	15	18	...

B

Term number (n)	1	2	3	4	5	6	...
Sequence	4	7	10	13	16	19	...

C

Term number (n)	1	2	3	4	5	6	...
Sequence	6	10	14	18	22	26	...

Ben wants to find the nth term of this linear sequence.

Term number (n)	1	2	3	4	5	...
Sequence	3	5	7	9	11	...

The terms go up by 2 each time.
The simplest sequence which does this is 2n. So I compare my sequence with 2n:

n	1	2	3	4	5	...
$2n$	2	4	6	8	10	
Sequence	3	5	7	9	11	...

$\Big)$ + 1

To get my sequence I have to add 1 to 2n, so its nth term is **2n + 1**.

E1 Find an expression for the nth term of each of these sequences.

(a)

n	1	2	3	4	5 ...
Sequence	10	13	16	19	22 ...

(b)

n	1	2	3	4	5 ...
Sequence	7	13	19	25	31 ...

E2 Find an expression for the nth term of each of these sequences.

(a) 1, 7, 13, 19, 25, 31, ...   (b) 4, 4.5, 5, 5.5, 6, 6.5, ...

(c) ⁻6, ⁻1, 4, 9, 14, 19, ...   (d) $5\frac{1}{4}$, $5\frac{1}{2}$, $5\frac{3}{4}$, 6, $6\frac{1}{4}$, $6\frac{1}{2}$, ...

E3 A pupil has tried to find the nth term of a linear sequence.

(a) Explain the mistake you think he has made.

(b) Find a correct expression for the nth term of the sequence.

8, 10, 12, 14, 16, ...
nth term is n + 2 ✗

E4 In a linear sequence, the difference between each term and the next is called the **constant difference.**

In the following problems, each sequence is linear.
Solve each problem, showing your method clearly.

1 My nth term is 5n – 6. What is my constant difference?

2 My constant difference is 6. My 4th term is 29. What is my nth term?

3 My 1st term is 1. My 20th term is 39. What is my nth term?

4 My 3rd term is 8. My 21st term is 17. What is my nth term?

5 My 15th term is 8 more than my 11th term. My 1st term is ⁻3. What is my nth term?

6 My 4th term is three times my 2nd term. My 6th term is a square number. What is my 3rd term?

Can you find more than one solution for this puzzle?

F Decreasing linear sequences

Ben wants to find the nth term of this decreasing sequence.

Term number (n)	1	2	3	4	5	...
Sequence	18	16	14	12	10	...

> The terms go down by 2 each time.
> The simplest sequence which does this is ^-2n. So I compare my sequence with ^-2n.
>
> | n | 1 | 2 | 3 | 4 | 5 | ... |
> |---|---|---|---|---|---|---|
> | ^-2n | $^-2$ | $^-4$ | $^-6$ | $^-8$ | $^-10$ | |
> | Sequence | 18 | 16 | 14 | 12 | 10 | ... |
>
> $+ 20$
>
> To get my sequence I have to add 20 to ^-2n, so its nth term is $^-2n + 20$ or $20 - 2n$.

F1 Find an expression for the nth term of each of these sequences.

(a)

n	1	2	3	4	...
Sequence	50	47	44	41	...

(b)

n	1	2	3	4	...
Sequence	100	99	98	97	...

F2 For each of the following linear sequences, find an expression for the nth term and calculate the 100th term.

(a) 98, 96, 94, 92, 90, ...   (b) 40, 34, 28, 22, 16, ...

(c) 50, 49.5, 49, 48.5, 48, ...   (d) 7, 6.8, 6.6, 6.4, 6.2, ...

What progress have you made?

Statement	Evidence
I can work out a formula from a design.	1 Pattern 2 Pattern 4 How many crosses are in the nth pattern?
I can use a rule for the nth term of a sequence.	2 The nth term of a sequence is $28 - 3n$. What is (a) the 6th term (b) the 10th term
I can find an expression for the nth term of an increasing linear sequence.	3 Find an expression for the nth term of (a) 11, 17, 23, 29, 35, ... (b) 2, 11, 20, 29, 38, ...
I can find an expression for the nth term of a decreasing linear sequence.	4 Find an expression for the nth term of 20, 17, 14, 11, 8, ...

23 Ratio

This is about using ratios to describe mixtures and to compare quantities.
The work will help you

- ◆ use the notation for ratio
- ◆ understand equal ratios
- ◆ share a quantity in a given ratio
- ◆ compare ratios

A Stronger, darker, sweeter, happier, …

For group then class discussion

1 Which of these recipes gives a stronger tasting drink?

2 Which of these recipes gives a darker shade of pink?

3 Which of these recipes gives a darker shade?

4 Which of these recipes gives a darker shade?

5 Which cup of tea will be sweeter?

A

B

300 ml

500 ml

6 Which family of piglets is happier?

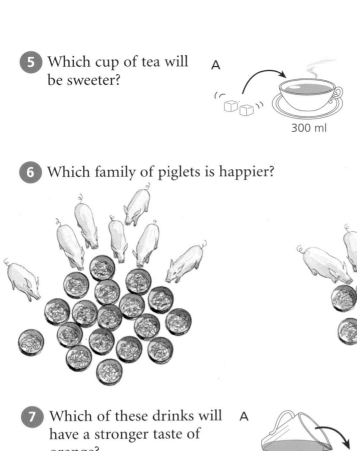

7 Which of these drinks will have a stronger taste of orange?

A

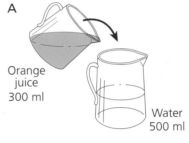

Orange juice 300 ml

Water 500 ml

B

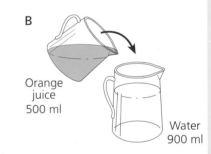

Orange juice 500 ml

Water 900 ml

8 Which of these gravies will have more flavour?

A

Water

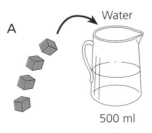

500 ml

B

Water

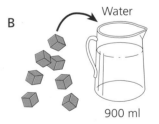

900 ml

9 Which hill is steeper?

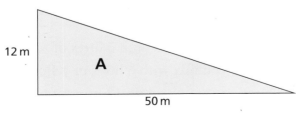

12 m

A

50 m

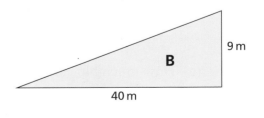

9 m

B

40 m

B Ratio notation

Here is a recipe for making light pink paint.

Light pink

Mix 4 tins of white with 1 tin of red.

You can make as much light pink paint as you like, but you must use 4 tins of white for every 1 tin of red you use.

The **ratio** of white to red is 4:1 (say '4 to 1').

The ratio of red to white is 1:4.

B1 You are making light pink paint from the recipe above.

   (a) How many tins of white do you mix with 3 tins of red?

   (b) How many tins of red do you mix with 20 tins of white?

B2 A recipe for light green says 'Mix blue and yellow in the ratio 2:5'.

Copy and complete this table of quantities.

Tins of blue	Tins of yellow
8	
14	
	25
	60

B3 Here is a recipe for dark green.

Dark green

Mix blue and yellow in the ratio 3:2.

   (a) How many tins of blue do you mix with 6 tins of yellow?

   (b) How many tins of yellow do you mix with 15 tins of blue?

   (c) If you want to make 50 litres of dark green, how many litres of blue and how many litres of yellow will you need?

B4

Muddy brown

Mix blue, yellow and red in the ratio 3:2:1.

   (a) How much blue and how much yellow do you mix with 5 litres of red?

   (b) How much blue and how much red do you mix with 6 litres of yellow?

   (c) How much yellow and how much red do you mix with 12 litres of blue?

C Darker, lighter

For pairs or small groups

If you mix red paint and yellow paint, you get orange.

If you mix a lot of red with a little of yellow, you get a dark orange.	If you mix a little of red with a lot of yellow, you get a light orange.

There are some recipes for orange colours below.

1 Sort the recipes according to how dark the orange will be.
(If there are any you can't decide on, put them in a separate list.)

2 How many different colours are there?

3 For each different colour, make up a new recipe which will give the same colour.

4 Make up a recipe for an orange colour which is somewhere between
two of the colours that can already be made.

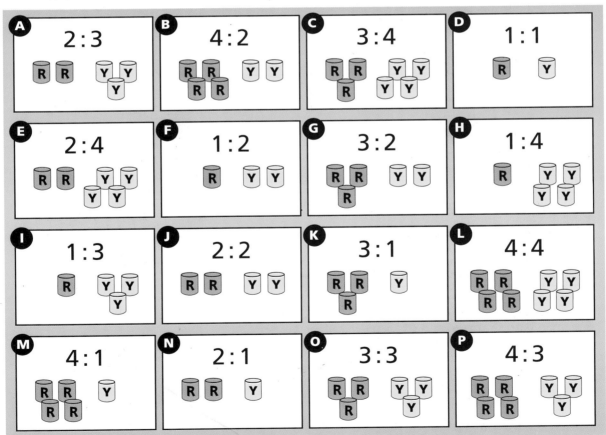

D Working with ratios

If we make orange by mixing 3 litres of red with 2 litres of yellow, the ratio of red to yellow is 3:2.

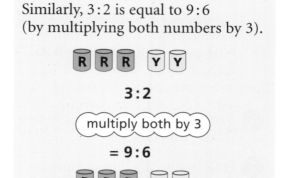

If we multiply both numbers by 2, we get the ratio 6:4.

The orange colour is the same.

We say that **3:2 is equal to 6:4**.

3:2

multiply both by 2

= 6:4

Similarly, 3:2 is equal to 9:6 (by multiplying both numbers by 3).

3:2

multiply both by 3

= 9:6

A ratio can sometimes be **simplified**.

9:6 can be simplified by **dividing** both numbers by 3.

So 9:6 is equal to 3:2, which is the **simplest form** of the ratio.

9:6

divide both by 3

= 3:2

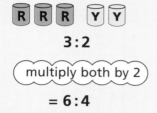

D1 A recipe for grass green says 'Mix blue and yellow in the ratio 3:1'.
  (a) How many litres of blue are mixed with 5 litres of yellow?
  (b) How many litres of yellow go with 30 litres of blue?

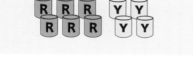

D2 A recipe for deep purple says 'Mix blue and red in the ratio 5:2'.
  (a) How many litres of blue go with 6 litres of red?
  (b) How many litres of red go with 10 litres of blue?

D3 When making concrete, you have to mix sand and gravel.
For every spadeful of sand you need 2 spadefuls of gravel.
  (a) Is the ratio of sand to gravel 2:1 or 1:2?
  (b) How many spadefuls of gravel go with 6 spadefuls of sand?
  (c) How many spadefuls of sand go with 40 spadefuls of gravel?

D4 Craig made a light green colour by mixing 20 litres of yellow with 5 litres of blue.
Write the ratio of yellow to blue in its simplest form.

D5 Dina made a pink colour by mixing 8 litres of red with 6 litres of white.
Write the ratio of red to white in its simplest form.

D6 Sergei made green by mixing 12 litres of blue with 9 litres of yellow.
  (a) Write the ratio of blue to yellow in its simplest form.
  (b) Write the ratio of yellow to blue in its simplest form.

D7 Write each of these ratios in its simplest form.
  (a) 9 : 3   (b) 15 : 10   (c) 20 : 30   (d) 8 : 14

D8 Sort these ratios into groups, so that the ratios in each group are equal.
In each group underline the simplest form.

1 : 5	4 : 6	3 : 1	4 : 20
3 : 2	20 : 100	12 : 8	9 : 3
12 : 4	2 : 3	10 : 15	2 : 10

D9 A recipe for pale green says 'Mix blue and yellow in the ratio 1 : 2'.
So 1 litre of blue and 2 litres of yellow will make 3 litres of pale green.

makes
3 pale green

Sharmila wants to make 30 litres of pale green.
How much blue and how much yellow should she use?

D10 Soft pink is made by mixing red and white in the ratio 1 : 3.
Kevin needs 20 litres of soft pink.
How much red and how much white should he use?

*D11 Grey paint is made by mixing black and white.
Here are the recipes for three kinds of grey.

  (a) Colin wants to make light grey.
      He has 3 litres of black.
      How much white does he need?

  (b) Sandra needs 30 litres of light grey.
      How much black and how much white does she need?

  (c) How much black and how much white are needed to make
      14 litres of medium grey?

  (d) You want to make medium grey.
      You already have 12 litres of black.
      How much white do you need?

  (e) How much black and how much white do you need
      to make 40 litres of dark grey?

Light grey

Mix black and white in the ratio 1 : 5

Medium grey

Mix black and white in the ratio 2 : 5

Dark grey

Mix black and white in the ratio 3 : 5

E Sharing in a given ratio

Paul and Karen have earned £20 between them.
Paul did more work, so they agree to share the money in the ratio **3:2**.

They think of Paul's share as 3 bags and Karen's as 2 bags.

Paul's share   Karen's share

   £20 altogether

There are 5 bags altogether.
Each bag must contain £20 ÷ 5 = £4.

So Paul gets 3 × £4 = **£12**

and Karen gets 2 × £4 = **£8**

Check: the total is £12 + £8 = £20.

E1 Stuart and Shula share £12 in the ratio 2:1. How much does each get?

E2 Dawn and Eve share £20 in the ratio 3:1. How much does each get?

E3 Beric and Betty share £21 in the ratio 3:4. How much does each get?

E4 Share each of these.
  (a) £20 in the ratio 4:1   (b) £60 in the ratio 2:3
  (c) £24 in the ratio 5:3   (d) £45 in the ratio 5:4
  (e) £12.50 in the ratio 3:2   (f) £6 in the ratio 3:1
  (g) £17.50 in the ratio 4:3   (h) £1.80 in the ratio 4:5

E5 James and Sarah's grandmother makes a will.
  When she dies, James and Sarah will have £2000 to share between them.
  They are to share it in the same ratios as their ages.

  (a) James is 3 and Sarah is 5. So if their grandmother dies now,
       they would share £2000 in the ratio 3:5.
       How much would each get?

  (b) How much would they each get if grandmother dies one year from now?
       Two years from now? Investigate further.

  (c) Who does better if grandmother lives longer?

E6 Alan, Bertha and Cyril share £300 in the ratio 1:2:3. How much does each get?

E7 (a) Share £13.50 in the ratio 2:3:4.

    (b) Share £66 in the ratio 2:3:7.

F Ratios in patterns

F1 This pattern of squares continues in both directions.

What is the ratio of blue to white squares in the pattern?

F2 Do the same for each of these patterns.

(a)

(b)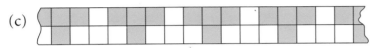

(c)

F3 This pattern continues in all directions.

What is the ratio of red to white squares in the pattern?

F4 Each of these patterns continues in all directions.

What is the ratio of coloured to white squares in each pattern?

(a)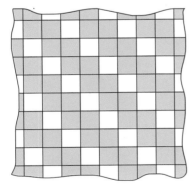

(b)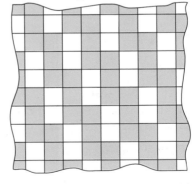

(c)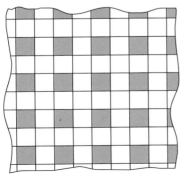

(d)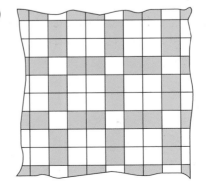

F5 You need sheet 190.

(a) What is the ratio of the number of octagons to the number of squares in this pattern?

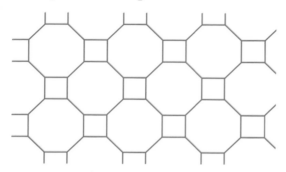

(b) What is the ratio of squares to equilateral triangles in this pattern?

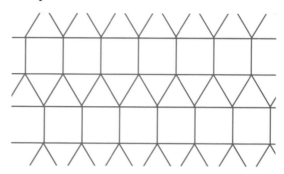

(c) What is the ratio of squares to triangles in this pattern?

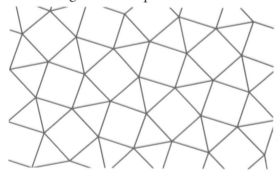

(d) What is the ratio of hexagons to triangles in this pattern?

(e) In this pattern, what is the ratio of
   (i)   hexagons to squares
   (ii) hexagons to triangles
   (iii) triangles to squares

G Comparing ratios

A ratio is unchanged when both numbers are multiplied or divided
by the same number.

This helps us to compare ratios.

Example

Royal pink is made by mixing red and white in the ratio $7:4$.
Festive pink is made by mixing red and white in the ratio $17:10$.

Which is the darker (that is, redder) pink?

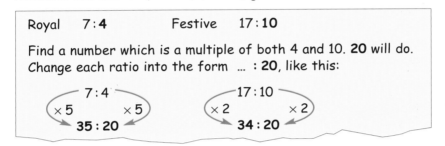

Royal $7:4$ Festive $17:10$

Find a number which is a multiple of both 4 and 10. **20** will do.
Change each ratio into the form … : **20**, like this:

G1 In the example above, which of the two pinks is darker?

G2 Find the missing numbers.

(a) $3:5 = \textbf{?}:25$ (b) $7:8 = \textbf{?}:32$ (c) $11:15 = \textbf{?}:90$ (d) $4:9 = 36:\textbf{?}$

G3 Find out which of these two grey colours is darker, and explain your method.

Squirrel grey   Mix black and white in the ratio $13:5$.
Thundercloud grey   Mix black and white in the ratio $8:3$.

G4 Jasmine made an orange drink by mixing 5 litres of juice with 8 litres of water.
Nita also made an orange drink but used 7 litres of juice and 11 litres of water.

Whose drink was stronger? Explain.

G5 Paul mixed 14 litres of apple juice with 9 litres of water.
Sue said the drink was too strong and added 2 litres of water.
David said that made it too weak, so he added 3 litres of apple juice.

Was the final drink stronger or weaker than to start with? Explain.

Challenge

In a bag there are red, green and blue marbles.
The ratio of red to green is $3:5$. The ratio of green to blue is $4:7$.

What is the ratio of red to blue?

H Writing a ratio as a single number

This rectangular window is 50 cm high and 20 cm wide.
The ratio **height : width** is 50 : 20, or 5 : 2.

Another way to write the ratio is as a division: $\dfrac{\textbf{height}}{\textbf{width}}$

So the ratio $\dfrac{\text{height}}{\text{width}} = \dfrac{50}{20} = \textbf{2.5}$

Written this way, the ratio is a **single number**.
The ratio 2.5 tells you that the height is 2.5 times the width.

height
50 cm

width
20 cm

H1 Calculate the ratio $\dfrac{\text{height}}{\text{width}}$ for each of these windows.

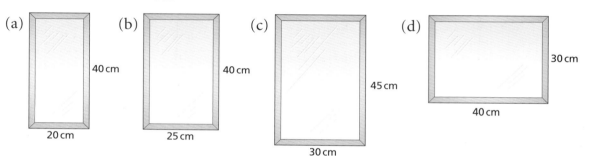

(a) 40 cm 20 cm

(b) 40 cm 25 cm

(c) 45 cm 30 cm

(d) 30 cm 40 cm

H2 If the ratio $\dfrac{\text{height}}{\text{width}}$ of a window is 1, what shape is the window?

H3 For each animal below, calculate the ratio $\dfrac{\text{weight of daily food intake}}{\text{body weight}}$.

Animal	Body weight	Weight of daily food intake
Hamster	125 g	25 g
Cat	3000 g	300 g
Elephant	5000 kg	20 kg

H4 For each of these hills, calculate
the ratio $\dfrac{\text{vertical distance}}{\text{horizontal distance}}$.

Which hill is steeper?

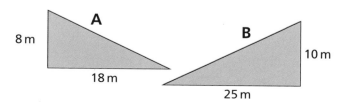

A 8 m 18 m

B 10 m 25 m

What progress have you made?

Statement

Evidence

I understand the way in which ratios are written.

1 Pale pink is made by mixing red and white in the ratio 2:5.

   (a) How much white do you mix with 8 litres of red?

   (b) How much red do you mix with 15 litres of white?

I can change a ratio into its simplest form.

2 Change each of these ratios to its simplest form.

   (a) 10:25   (b) 16:24

I can share a quantity in a given ratio.

3 Gavin and Susan share £36 in the ratio 4:5.

   How much does each get?

4 Peter, Paul and Mary share £100 in the ratio 1:3:4.

   How much does each get?

I can compare ratios.

5 Which of these recipes will give a darker shade of grey? Explain your answer.

   A: Mix black and white in the ratio 5:8

   B: Mix black and white in the ratio 3:5

I can calculate a ratio as a single number.

6 Calculate the ratio $\dfrac{\text{vertical distance}}{\text{horizontal distance}}$ for this hill.

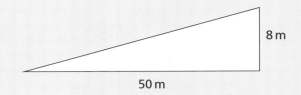

8 m

50 m

Using a spreadsheet

This work will help you use a spreadsheet to solve problems.

Notation $*$ stands for $\times$ $/$ stands for $\div$ $\wedge$ stands for a power ($3\wedge2$ means 3^2)

Formulas in spreadsheets start with =.

The formula = **2*A1** works out $2 \times$ the number in A1.

Spot the formula   For pairs of pupils

The first person puts a number into cell **A1**.
Then they put a formula into another cell.

	A	B
1	10	
2		
3	= 3*A1 + 12	
4		
5		

Now they just click in
another cell.

	A	B
1	10	
2		
3	42	
4		
5		

The second person has to try to find out the
formula by trying different numbers in **A1**.

When they think they know the formula,
they type it into the spreadsheet.

	A	B
1	10	
2		
3	42	
4		= 4*A1 + 2
5		

They check they are right by
trying some more numbers
in **A1**.

	A	B
1	5	*Oh blow!*
2		
3	27	
4		22
5		

Challenge

The second person has to find a formula that undoes the first person's.

So in the example above, the undoing formula would start with 42 and produce 10.

Making a sequence

Type 1, 2, 3, 4, …
into the first
column.

	A	B
1	1	
2	2	
3	3	
4	4	
5	5	
	6	

Find a formula
you can **fill down**
to get this
sequence.

	A	B
1	1	1
2	2	3
3	3	5
4	4	7
5	5	9
	6	11

Now see if you can find a formula you can fill down to get each of these.

1

1	2
2	4
3	6
4	8
5	10
6	12
7	14

2

1	2
2	5
3	8
4	11
5	14
6	17
7	20

3

1	6
2	11
3	16
4	21
5	26
6	31
7	36

4

1	1
2	4
3	9
4	16
5	25
6	36
7	49

5

1	0
2	3
3	8
4	15
5	24
6	35
7	48

6

1	1
2	3
3	6
4	10
5	15
6	21
7	28

Big, bigger, biggest

Set up your spreadsheet like this.

	A	B
1		2
2		3
3		5
4		4
5		
6	Sum	?
7		
8	Product	?
9		

You can type any four numbers into these four cells.

Put a formula in this cell that adds up to your four numbers.

Put a formula here that multiplies your four numbers together.

1 (a) Can you find four numbers whose sum is 14 and whose product is 84?

(b) Find four numbers with a sum of 14 and a product of 108.

(c) What is the largest product you can find with four numbers whose sum is 14?

2 (a) Can you find four numbers whose sum is 15 and whose product is 180?

(b) Find four numbers with a sum of 15 and a product of 137.5.

(c) Find the largest product you can get with four numbers that add up to 15.

Ways and means

Put two numbers into your spreadsheet, one above the other.

	A	B
1		
2		
3		2
4		8
5		
6		
7		
8		

Put a formula to find the mean of the two numbers into the next cell.

	A	B
1		
2		
3		2
4		8
5		5
6		
7		
8		

Drag and drop the formula down the column.

	A	B
1		
2		
3		2
4		8
5		5
6		6.5
7		5.75
8		6.125

- What do you notice?
- Investigate how the numbers you start with affect the result.
- Investigate what happens when you start with three numbers and find their mean. What about four numbers?

Parcel volume

Parcel Force have a rule about the biggest sized parcel you can send.

It depends on the length and the girth of the parcel. (The girth is the distance all the way round it.)

PARCEL DELIVERY

Individual parcels can weight up to 30 kg, with a maximum length of 1.5 m and a total of 3 m when length and girth are combined.

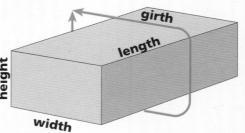

What is the largest volume of parcel you can send?
Set up a spreadsheet to investigate this.
One way to organise it might be like this.

	A	B	C	D	E	F
1	Height	Width	Length	Girth	Length+Girth	Volume
2						

Furry festivals

Furry sell souvenirs at festivals.
They sell T-shirts, badges and pens.

At one festival they sold 60 items altogether.
(They sold at least one of everything.)
They took £200 for the items.

Use a spreadsheet to help you work out how many of each item they sold.
Is there only one answer?

Furry festivals
T-shirts £22
Badges £2
Pens £1

Put here the number of T-shirts you think they sold.

Put a formula here for the cost of the T-shirts.

	A	B	C	D	E	
1						
2		Cost each (£)	Number		Total cost (£)	
3	T-shirts	22				
4	Badges	2				
5	Pens	1				
6						
7		Total number		Grand total		
8						

Put formulas here for the cost of badges and pens.

Put here the number of items they sold.

Put a formula here for the cost of all the items they sold.

Breakfast time

Foods contain different proportions of protein, carbohydrate and fat, as shown, for example, in the table below.

Food	% protein	% carbohydrate	%fat	Amount (g)
Cornflakes	8	25	0.7	
Milk	3	5	4	
White bread	8	4	2	
Butter	0.5	0	82	
Jam	0.6	69	0	

Put the table into a spreadsheet and enter these amounts.

Cornflakes 30 g
Milk 150 g
White bread 120 g
Butter 5 g
Jam 10 g

Add three extra columns 'Amount of protein', 'Amount of carbohydrate', 'Amount of fat'. Use suitable formulas to find the total amounts of protein, fat and carbohydrate in the breakfast above.

Mean, median, range

We can use a spreadsheet to find the mean, median and range of a set of numbers.

	A	B
1	Ben	1
2	Priya	13
3	David	4
4	Maddi	17
5	Sorayah	6
6	Martin	15
7	Jenny	10
8	Paul	11
9	April	2
10	Will	20
11		
12	Mean	9.9
13	Median	10.5
14	Range	19

1 The data on the right shows the number of cans collected by a class.

Set this up on a spreadsheet.

12	Mean	=AVERAGE (B1:B10)
13	Median	=MEDIAN (B1:B10)
14	Range	=MAX (B1:B10) – MIN (B1:B10)

You can use formulas like this in cells B12, B13 and B14.

2 Can you predict what will happen to the mean, median and range if

(a) Will got 200 not 20

(b) David found 2 more cans

(c) 8 of Priya's cans had to be thrown away

(d) Martin has to give 6 of his cans to David

Try out your ideas.
(This will probably be easier if you make a copy of column B.)

3 What will happen to the mean, median and range if

(a) the pupils each had ten cans added

(b) they each had two cans taken away

(c) the school got 5p per can, so the numbers were multiplied by five

Work out some rules about what happens when you add, multiply or subtract numbers to all the data.

4 By changing just one number in the data above, find sets of 10 numbers with these values.

(a) Mean 10   Median 10.5   Range 19

(b) Mean 11   Median 10.5   Range 23

(c) Mean 9   Median 8   Range 19

(d) Mean 11.1   Median 12   Range 21

25 Functions and graphs

This work will help you

◆ draw the graph of a function like $y = 2x + 3$

◆ find the equation of a straight line graph

A From table to graph

Teacher-led discussion

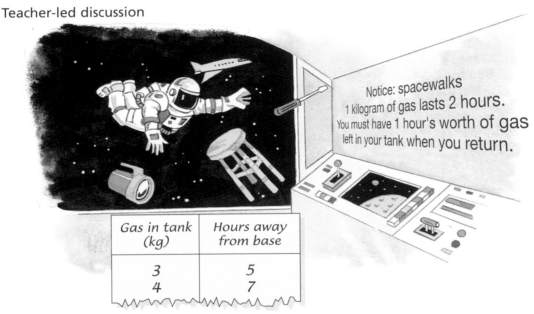

Gas in tank (kg)	Hours away from base
3	5
4	7

A1 (a) The table above shows how many hours you can be away from base.
Complete the table up to at least 9 kilograms.

(b) Plot the points from your table on graph paper.
The points should all lie on a straight line.
Draw the line through the points.

(c) Suppose you have $4\frac{1}{2}$ kg of gas in your tank.
Use the graph to find how many hours you can be away from base.

(d) You want to be away from base for 10 hours.
How many kg of gas should you put in your tank?

(e) Suppose you have a giant tank with 100 kg of gas in it.
How long can you stay away from base?

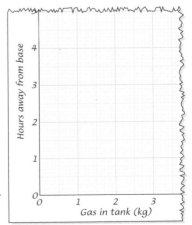

A2 Petra sees a snail crawling up a post.
When she first sees it, it is 20 cm from the ground.

She measures its height from the ground every hour and finds that it climbs 30 cm in each hour.

(a) Copy and complete this table, showing the time that has passed in hours (t) and the height of the snail in cm (h).

t	0	1	2	3	4	5	6
h	20	50					

(b) There is a formula connecting h and t.
Work out what it is and write it as $h = \ldots$

(c) Draw a graph to show the time that has passed and the snail's height in centimetres.

(d) Use the graph to find t when $h = 100$.

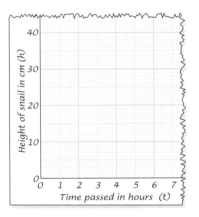

A3 The ground clearance of a vehicle is the distance between the bottom of the vehicle and the ground.

For this lorry there is a formula for the ground clearance.

It is $d = 100 - 5w$

d is the ground clearance in centimetres.
w is the weight, in tonnes, the lorry is carrying.

(a) Copy and complete this table of values of w and d.

w	0	2	4	6	8	10
d	100				60	

(b) Draw axes on graph paper with w across and d up and plot the points from the table. They should lie on a straight line.
Draw the line and label it '$d = 100 - 5w$'.

(c) Use the graph to find the value of w for which $d = 77$.

(d) The lorry should not be driven if the ground clearance is less than 65 cm.
What is the maximum weight the lorry can carry?

B Functions

You can think of the equation $y = 2x + 1$ as a rule, or **function**, linking x and y.

For each value of x, you can find the value of y.

Here is a **table of values** of x and y.

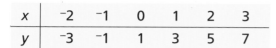

x	-2	-1	0	1	2	3
y	-3	-1	1	3	5	7

When you plot x and y as coordinates, the points lie on a straight line.

This line is the **graph** of $y = 2x + 1$.

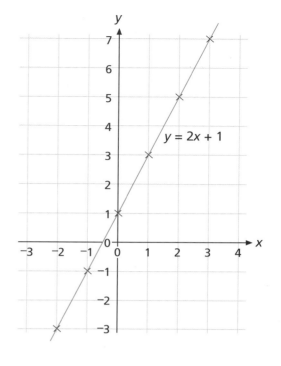

Draw axes with x and y from $^-6$ to 6.
Draw all the graphs in the following questions on the same set of axes.

B1 (a) Copy and complete this table of values for the function $y = x + 1$.

x	-6	-4	-2	0	2	4	6
y	-5						

(b) Plot the points from the table.
Draw and label the graph of $y = x + 1$.

B2 (a) Copy and complete this table of values for the function $y = 2x - 3$.

x	-1	0	1	2	3	4
y						

(b) Plot the points from the table.
Draw and label the graph of $y = 2x - 3$.

B3 (a) Copy and complete this table of values for the function $y = 2 - x$.

x	-4	-2	0	2	4	6
y						

(b) Plot the points from the table.
Draw and label the graph of $y = 2 - x$.

B4 Make your own table of values for the function $y = 5 - 2x$.
Draw and label the graph of $y = 5 - 2x$.

201

C Spot the function

This activity is described in the teacher's guide.

Nina's rule was $y = 2x - 6$.
Here are some of her points.

x	y
3	0
4	2
6	6
11	16

Here are some of the points for Luke's rule.

x	y
0	2
2	8
3	11
4	14

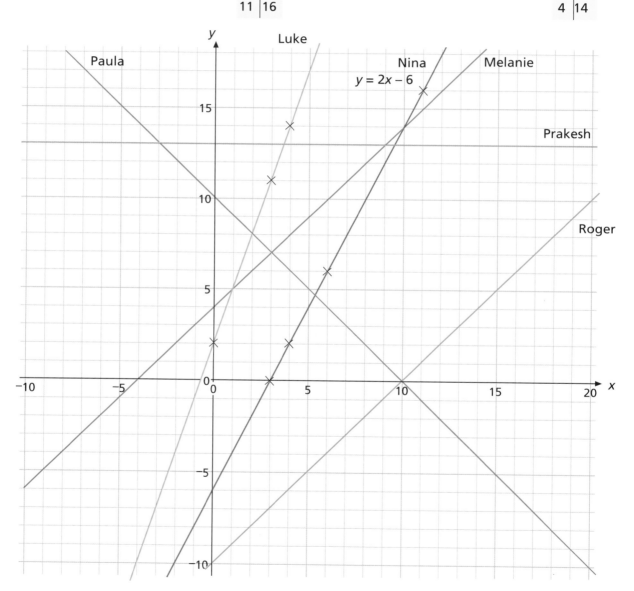

C1 Look at the graph for Luke's rule.
Copy and complete this table of coordinates for points on the graph.

x	0	1	2	3	4
y	2	5	8		

As x goes up by 1, so y goes up by 3 each time.
So the equation connecting y and x is either $y = 3x + $ a number,
or $y = 3x - $ a number.

Find the equation for Luke's graph.

C2 One person's rule was $x + y = 10$.
Copy and complete this table of coordinates for this rule.

x	0	1	2	3	4
y	10				

Find the line that goes through these points and say who used this rule.

C3 What rule did Melanie use? (It may help to make a table of the coordinates of some of the points on the graph.)

C4 One person used the rule $y = 13$. So whatever value of x he was given, he always said '13' for the value of y.

What is his name?

C5 What rule did Roger use?

C6 Find the equation of each of the lines shown here.

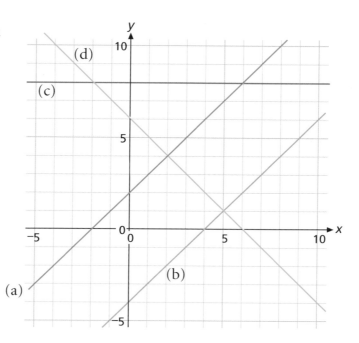

C7 Dina did an experiment with a spring. She hung different weights from the spring and measured its length.

She drew the graph on the right to show her results.

Find a formula linking L and W.

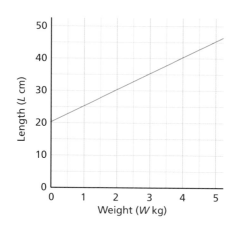

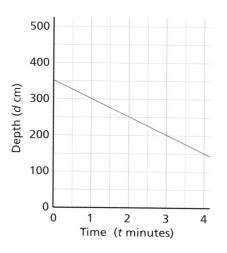

C8 A water tank is being emptied.

The graph on the left shows the depth, d cm, of the water after the tap has been open for t minutes.

Find a formula linking d and t.

*C9 Find the equation of each of the lines shown here.

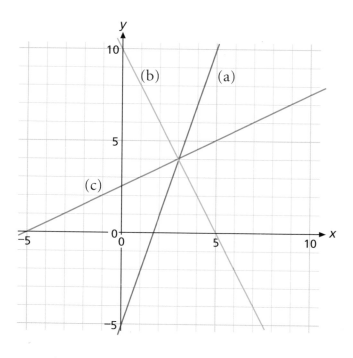

*C10 Temperatures can be measured in degrees Celsius (°C) or degrees Fahrenheit (°F).
To convert a temperature from °C to °F you use the formula

$$F = 1.8C + 32$$

F is the temperature in °F; C is the temperature in °C.

(a) Copy and complete this table of values.

C	⁻15	⁻10	⁻5	0	5	10	15	20
F	5							

(b) Draw axes with C across and F up.
Use 1 cm to stand for 10 degrees on both axes.

Plot the points from your table.
Draw and label the graph of $F = 1.8C + 32$.

(c) A rough rule for converting from Celsius to Fahrenheit is

$$F = 2C + 30$$

Draw the graph of this equation on the same axes.

(d) For which value of C does the rough rule give the correct value of F?

(e) Between which values of C does the rough rule give a value of F which
is within 5°F of the correct value?

What progress have you made?

Statement	Evidence
I can draw the graph of a function like $y = 2x + 3$.	1 Draw the graph of the function $y = 2x + 3$, for values of x from ⁻4 to 4.
I can find the equation of a straight line graph.	2 Find the equation of each line below.

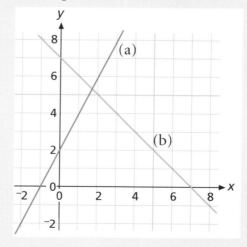

Review 3

1 Evaluate each of these.

(a) $0.862 + \dfrac{0.94^2}{2.5}$

(b) $\dfrac{3.48 + 2.74}{\sqrt{3.24} + 2.2}$

(c) $6.16 - \dfrac{(^-3.72 - ^-1.45)}{1.6^2}$

2 The diagram shows a prism. Calculate

(a) its volume

(b) its surface area

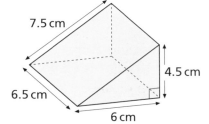

7.5 cm

6.5 cm

6 cm

4.5 cm

3 (a) Find a formula for the nth term of each of these sequences.

(i) 3, 9, 15, 21, 27, ...

(ii) 46, 42, 38, 34, 30, ...

(b) Calculate the 20th term of each of the sequences.

4 Simplify each of these expressions where possible.

(a) $7 - 2a + 3 + 8a$

(b) $2 \times 4b \times 3b$

(c) $3c - 11 - 5c + 6$

(d) $8 + 5d$

(e) $e - 1 - e + 4$

(f) $f \times 2 \times 7f$

5 Jane and Sinead are learning to use a bow and arrows.
Jane hit the target in 15 shots out of 23, Sinead in 19 shots out of 30.
Use percentages to find out who did better.

6 I think of a number, multiply it by 2.5, add 1.5, divide by 0.5 and subtract 4.5.
The result is 38.5. What number did I think of?

7 During dry weather, the depth of water in a reservoir goes down
by 2 metres each day.
The water is 25 metres deep at the start of a dry spell.

(a) Copy and complete this table.

Number of days after start, t	0	1	2	3	4	5	6
Depth of water in metres, d	25	23					

(b) Plot the points from the table on a graph.
Draw the straight line through the points.

(c) What is the formula linking d and t? Write it in the form $d = \ldots$

(d) If the dry spell continues, after how many days will the reservoir be empty?

8 Look at this sequence: 16, 24, 36, 54, ...

   (a) The ratio *first term* : *second term* is 16:24. Write this in its simplest form.

   (b) Write the ratio *second term* : *third term* in its simplest form.

   (c) Do the same for the ratio *third term* : *fourth term.*

   (d) The sequence continues in the same way, so that the ratio of each term to the next term is always the same. Work out the next two terms.

9 Solve each of these equations.

   (a) $5n - 14 = 31$ (b) $3(n + 17) = 30$ (c) $\dfrac{n}{4} + 26 = 61$

10 What is the equation of each of these straight line graphs?

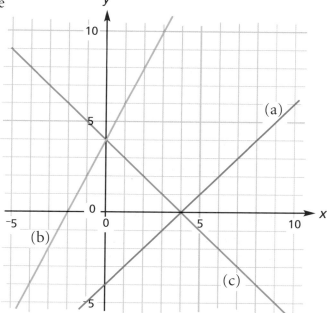

11 What is the ratio of coloured to white squares in each of these infinite patterns?

   (a)

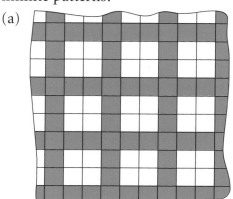

   (b)

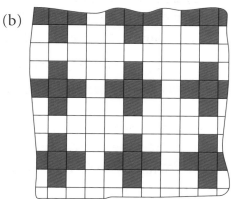

12 Write these fractions and decimals in order of size, starting with the smallest.

$$\frac{17}{50} \quad \frac{2}{5} \quad 0.37 \quad \frac{8}{25} \quad 0.3 \quad \frac{1}{4} \quad \frac{7}{20} \quad \frac{39}{100}$$

13 Calculate the angles marked with letters, giving reasons.

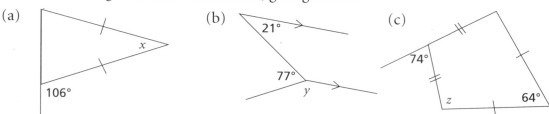

(a)   (b)   (c)

14 This is an 'addition cross'.
The numbers across make an addition sum: 7 + 2 = 9
So do the numbers down: 4 + 2 = 6

(a) Add together the numbers in the red squares.
Add together the numbers in the blue squares.
What do you find?

(b) Make some more addition crosses and do the same.

(c) Explain the result by using letters
to stand for these three numbers.

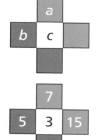

(d) Investigate 'multiplication crosses',
such as this one.

15 There are 60 small cubes in this cuboid.
Its dimensions are 5 by 6 by 2.

How many different cuboids can be made with 60 cubes?
(2 by 5 by 6 counts the same as 5 by 6 by 2.)

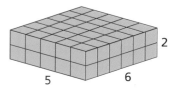

16 This diagram shows a square garden 16 m by 16 m.
There is a pathway, of constant width, round the edge.

The area of the square lawn inside the pathway is
half the total area of the garden.

Calculate the width of the path, correct to two
decimal places.

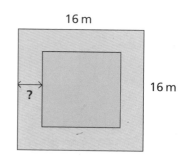